Words Fail Me

My Years in Ghana

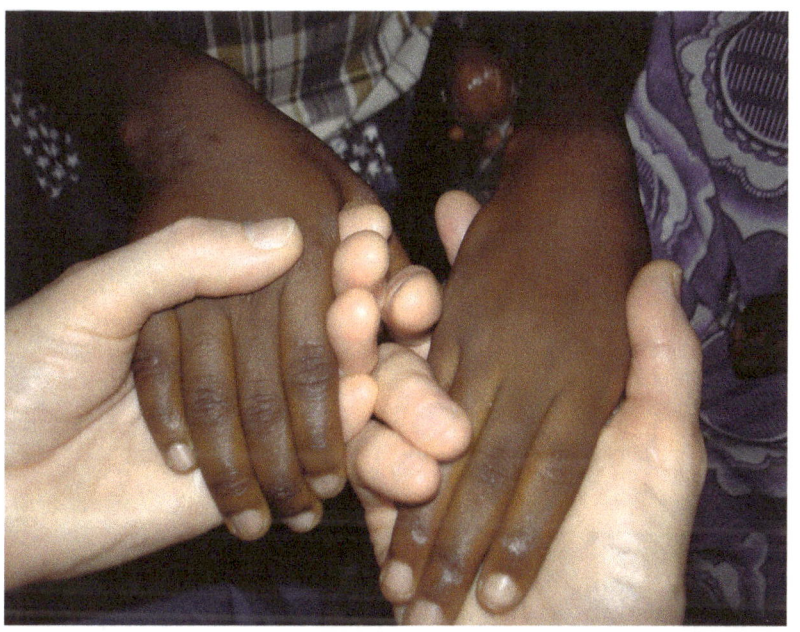

Carole Tanney

Words Fail Me

Copyright © 2019 Carole Tanney
ISBN 978-1-896213-96-5 POD
ISBN 978-1-896213-97-2 E-book

PUBLISHED IN CANADA
byDesign Media
www.bydesignmedia.ca

COVER & INTERIOR DESIGN — Diane Roblin-Lee

Disclaimer: The opinions expressed in this book are those of the author and do not constitute part of the curriculum of any program. The development, preparation and publication of this work has been undertaken with great care. However, the author, publisher and editors are not responsible for any errors contained herein or for consequences that may ensue from use of materials or information contained in this work. The information contained herein does not constitute legal or medical advice. References to quoted sources are only as current as the date of the publications. Where any sourced material may have been inadequately referenced, the author extends a apology. All rights reserved. No part of this publication may be reproduced, stored in a retrieval system, or transmitted in any form or by any means without prior permission of the Copyright owner.

All profits go to *World Hope International* (Canada), designated for Ghana.

Contents

Foreword—Rev. Joe Ocran	p. 5
Foreword—Laurence Croswell	p. 7
Introduction	p. 9
Chapter 1 How it All Started	p. 13
Chapter 2 Ghana Clinic Thursday, May 27, 1993	p. 21
Chapter 3 Tribal Customs	p. 25
Chapter 4 Known by Your Name	p. 31
Chapter 5 Customs Experiences	p. 33
Chapter 6 1994 Trip	p. 37
Chapter 7 The First Team—1995	p. 41
Chapter 8 1996 Luggage Problem?	p. 49
Chapter 9 1997- New Mitsubishi Van—Mobile Clinic	p. 53
Chapter 10 Ghana's First Scholarship Student	p. 61
Chapter 11 The TripFrom Hell—1999	p. 67
Chapter 12 The CIDA Youth Internship Program	p. 73
Chapter 13 The History of the Klefe Vocational School	p. 79
Chapter 14 What Good is a One Day Clinic?	p. 83
Chapter 15 Very Memorable 2002 Trip	p. 87
Chapter 16 A Life-Long Dream—2003	p. 93
Chapter 17 2004—Death Seems to be Following Us	p. 101
Chapter 18 We Need a Dentist—2005 Team	p. 107
Chapter 19 Elephant at My Door! Kanata Team—2005	p. 113
Chapter 20 The Kingston Team—2006	p. 121
Chapter 21 The Second Dental Team—2007	p. 129
Chapter 22 Visitors and Conference—2009	p. 143

Chapter 23	Here—Take My Child	p. 151
Chapter 24	Hurry up and Wait! 2011	p. 153
Chapter 25	Ghana and Burkina Faso—2014 Team	p. 161
Chapter 26	A Male-Dominated Team—2015	p. 171
Chapter 27	Two Tiny Problems	p. 185
Chapter 28	I Can't Find My.... 2017	p. 191
Chapter 29	Twentieth Trip—2018	p. 201
Chapter 30	Where to Go From Here	p. 213
Project Reach Out		p. 217

Foreword – Rev. Joe Ocran

Carole Tanney and my family have been friends for over thirty years. In 1992 the board of *Project Reach Out Canada* (NGO) invited Carole to be the chairperson, and she graciously accepted the challenge. The aim of *Project Reach Out* was to provide humanitarian help to the vulnerable people in Ghana and beyond, in support of the evangelization and church planting work of the Christian Standard Ministries, (The Wesleyan Church, Ghana).

As the daughter of a preacher and missionary, Carole approached her role with passion and the importance that it deserved. In 1993, after only a year of taking office, Carole undertook her maiden visit to Ghana to acquaint herself with projects started by our NGO—and most importantly—to get to know the people we serve and the country of Ghana. This was to be the beginning of about twenty trips to Ghana (so far) made by Carole.

This lady continues to be a great friend of my family. For the first few years after my family moved to Ghana, Carole was our link to Canada. She wrote letters which always included top news items in Canada, even sports news.

Carole is very passionate about getting help to those in need, and brought dynamism and much needed leadership to an otherwise floundering organization. On her visits Carole always carried a journal and therefore kept records of her experiences. It came as no surprise to me when she decided to write this book, detailing her twenty-six years (and counting) of work and travels in Ghana. Carole tells me stories of our encounters and adventures that I have long forgotten, but which are fresh in her journals or memory.

I trust that you will enjoy reading this book through the lens provided by Carole.

Rev. Joe Ocran
Missionary to Ghana
Retired National Superintendent of Wesleyan Church Ghana

Foreword – Laurence Croswell

During my forty years of pastoring The Brockville Standard Church / Centennial Road Church (1968—2008), I have seen some of the people there become influencers and history makers with their involvement and ministries. Such a person was Carole Tanney. Never content to just sit by and not be involved, Carole began a music ministry with us as church pianist, ultimately increasing her involvement by becoming choir director for special cantatas and occasions as well. When music styles began to change in the 1980's, Carole switched her involvement to a much wider and more influential ministry: she became director of *Project Reach Out*, organizing fund raisers and conducting ministry tours to serve our pioneer work in Ghana, Africa under the leadership of Rev. Joe and Jemima Ocran. Since that time, Carole has seen the work in Ghana grow from one church to over forty preaching points with a national superintendent. Carole has demonstrated a lifetime of service that abounds with energetic service to her Lord Jesus Christ and His Church. Her story will inspire and challenge you to greater service and love for Jesus!

Laurence Croswell
Western Canada Ministries, The Wesleyan Church

Introduction

What is that noise I hear? Is it laughing, arguing, or crying? Oh! It's my friends all talking and laughing when they read the title of this book! *A book written by Carole Tanney called Words Fail Me? It can't be! Words have never failed Carole. Of all the people we know she is the last one who could say that words fail her.*

So many surprising things have happened during the twenty-five years I have been traveling to Ghana that when I try to put them down on paper, words *do* fail me.

The words of the title of this book were spoken by the chief of a Muslim village when I tried to explain why we had come to his village, working all day in the heat to treat his people free of charge. You will find the story of those events in Chapter Twenty-one.

At the start of each mission trip, we held meetings with the *Ghana Project Reach Out (PRO)* board to prioritize needs for the trip. Upon our return home, we reported to the Canadian board of *PRO* regarding the decisions and recommendations of the Ghana Board and the accomplishments of the teams. During the *CIDA* funding years, we provided reports on all the projects they were funding.

Crystal River sings a song I like called, "Thank You Says It Best." The message is that we'll never understand why God loves us and why we are so blessed. When words fail *us*, like

Crystal River, we find that "Thank You" says it best. This is my mantra at this time in my life. I could have gone so many ways, but I decided to follow God's leading and get involved in the Ghana mission efforts. I never imagined it would go on for so long and take the route that it has. Even though I always have something to say, there truly are times when I feel there aren't enough words to describe adequately how I feel.

There are so many people to thank! First of all, all my thanks go to God for giving me the all the opportunities to get involved in the ministry in Ghana. After my ministry in music was finished and my disappointment led me to feel I was no longer useful in the church, Sherrie Davis sat me down and said "God isn't finished with you yet. He will multiply your ministry more than you can imagine," and that has come to pass. Thanks for the encouragement, Sherrie.

All the board members of *Project Reach Out Canada* over the years were very supportive and willing to go above and beyond when it came to praying for the work and volunteering for fundraising events. It is impossible to mention all the volunteers by name but each of you has contributed not only to the success of the work in Ghana but also to my personal success over the years. A huge thank you to each of you.

My parents' adventurous spirits certainly made an impression on me, doing different types of ministry and living "outside the box" when the things they did were frowned upon by the established church at the time. My husband, Lorne, was beyond tolerant with the things I wanted to do. He liked to travel, and we did some of that, but he never wanted to go to Ghana. He said he could stand neither the heat nor the fact that being on time was not a priority in the culture of Ghana. He was adamant about always being on time, even early, for every occasion. Fortunately, my adult children were both very supportive of my missionary travels.

Joe and Jemima Ocran were the creators of *Project Reach Out* and initiated the Christian Standard Church in Ghana and then the transition to join with the Wesleyan Church Ghana. I came into *Project Reach Out* two years after it started. After I became chairperson in 1993, in collaboration with Joe and Jemima, we implemented many of our new ideas. Joe and Jemima explained the ideas and convinced people in Ghana of the value of the changes, and that could not have been an easy job! There were government officials to convince and many reports to write, but we accomplished it all. Building infrastructure required the purchase of property, rental of equipment, and hiring of people, all in a timely manner that must have stretched the resources and patience of those in Ghana. I appreciate all the work done over the years by Joe and Jemima, by Joe's secretary, Faustina Yalley, and all their staff and coworkers. I have developed a great love for them over the years and thank them and their families for their thoughtfulness and kindness.

So many people have encouraged me, prayed for me and supported me over the years of the work with *Project Reach Out Canada* and recently with *World Hope International* (Canada). Thank you to all of you.

Also thank you to Kathy deSouza and Joe Ocran for their assistance in editing the text. My grammar, spelling, and composition were greatly enhanced by Kathy's teacher's eye. Joe gave help with Ghanaian customs and traditions and his recollection of events. Thanks to both of you.

Lastly, thanks to my publisher, Diane Roblin-Lee (byDesign Media) for all her work and her willingness to take this manuscript from a novice author and bring it to fruition.

Chapter 1

How it All Started

My family was very missions minded. My great aunt, Mrs. Naomi Green, founded the *Women's Missionary Society* of the Standard Church of America, the church where my parents were members. Monthly missionary meetings often featured missionaries home on furlough or retired missionaries as speakers. I regularly went to these meetings.

After my father became a minister in the Standard Church, these missionaries often stayed in our home where I was fascinated to hear the stories of their work.

When my parents retired from active pastoral ministry, they went to Egypt as Volunteers In Service Abroad (VISA) missionaries with the Free Methodist Church. In January 1981, I went to visit them in Egypt and got my first taste of hands-on missions work.

I became friends with Joe and Jemima Ocran when they came to Brockville for theological training at Brockville Bible College before returning to their home country of Ghana. Before they returned to Ghana in 1990, they founded *Project Reach Out* as the humanitarian arm of the ministry of the church in Ghana. A *Project Reach Out* board was established in Canada to provide prayer and financial support for the *Project Reach Out* board in Ghana.

In October of 1992, a Missionary Convention was held in the Ottawa Standard Church. I had recently joined the *Project Reach Out Canada* board and went to the conference as their representative. It was a moving conference, and I felt a definite "tugging" of my heart that God was calling me to go to Ghana to visit the mission. Up until that time, Rev. Earl Conley had been the only person from Canada to visit the mission. I talked to my pastor, Rev. Laurence Croswell, about this and, after a time of prayer about it, he encouraged me to plan to go to Ghana.

May twentieth, 1993 saw me boarding a plane in Toronto for my first trip to Ghana. My parents were at the airport waiting to board a flight on one of their holidays, and we coincidentally ended up in the same boarding lounge. In those days, smoking was allowed on airplanes. I sat in the last row of the non-smoking seats—so I might as well have been in the smoking section!

The trip from Toronto through Amsterdam to Ghana is 11,214 kilometres and, on average, takes approximately seven hours flying time to Amsterdam with a six to eight hour wait in the airport in Amsterdam; then approximately seven to eight hours more to Ghana. This makes for a tiring, long trip! I often broke up the wait in Amsterdam by going on a canal tour or doing a walking tour around interesting sites in the city.

It was a long trip, and I was the only white person in the section of the flight to Accra. A drunken man on the plane caused quite a commotion being very bothersome to all the passengers. The staff ended up shackling him hand and foot for the last half of the flight. When we deplaned and went to the luggage carousel, this man with his police escort stood right beside me every place I went! Joe finally came into the area and stood between the man and me.

Even though I was very tired from travelling, I was fascinated by the drive to the Ocran's home in Tema. Night markets were open all along the road with the kerosene lamps hanging on their stalls and people shopping in the dark. It was May twenty-first, my birthday, when I actually landed in Ghana; the Ocrans had a birthday party for me when we arrived at their house at ten-thirty at night. I was so tired that I could hardly talk, but we had chocolate cake and presents before I went to bed.

A wonderful welcome to the Christian Standard Church.

The roosters started at four-thirty a.m., and people were up and talking at five a.m. The power was off, so we had no fans and no refrigerator. Dinner was cooked outside on a charcoal stove. It was very hot. The best place was sitting on the balcony outside of Joe and Jemima's bedroom. If there was a breeze from the sea, it was there.

When it rains here, it really rains! I heard a noise that sounded like a train and asked Jemima how far away the train tracks were. She said there was no train. *Well, what is the noise I hear?* She listened and said it was the rain coming, beating on the tin roofs of the houses. Sure enough, it started to pour. When the rain hit the ground and the cement driveway, it bounced back, and the combination of the rain coming down and the splatter coming back up made it impossible to see anything!

The Ocrans at Community Nine Church, Tema

The weekly routine included Sunday School, church, prayer meeting, and choir practice. Wednesday assemblies were held at Community Nine school for three hundred students in the morning and another three hundred in the afternoon. The school couldn't accommodate all the students at the same time, so the morning session was from seven a.m. until noon, and the afternoon session was from one p.m. to six. Families who could afford to pay the school fees and pay for uniforms as well as school books and necessities could send their children to school. If they could not afford it, their children stayed at home. Many children were on the streets. Joe and Jemima ministered to people wherever they were. They knocked on doors, talked to people on the streets, and visited homes and hospitals.

It is impossible to relate everything that happened in the four weeks I was in Ghana. There were so many physical, educational, medical, and spiritual needs that words fail me! I was able to tour the Tema General Hospital and get a taste of the developing world's medical care—an eye-opening experience. When a patient is admitted to the hospital, they pay for the bed and the nursing care; no money—no bed or care. There are no linens and there is no food. The family has to bring it in or stay at the hospital and cook. There are no medicines unless someone can go to the pharmacy and pay for them in advance.

Impressions From My First Visit

- Jemima's purse is always open. Everyone wants something, and it is usually money for food for their family, for bus fare, for their many needs
- Women get up about five a.m. to do housework before it gets hot. This includes sweeping the property and cutting what grass there is with a machete
- There were no other white people around. I finally saw a family of "obrunis" (white people) in my third week there
- Children called me "the big white lady"
- We had to shop often as the power was off and the refrigerator didn't work well
- All women work both at home and outside the home—selling on the streets and markets, baking bread, selling porridge, sewing, farming, going for water and wood and carrying it home on their heads
- Trying to get the pulpit from the carpenter to the Ashalley-Botwe church. The tailgate wouldn't close, so we had to tie it and drive over the red dirt roads to get there. I looked at Jemima, and she looked at me, and we started to laugh. We were both covered in red dirt—so funny!

- Jemima's bird—every morning at ten after five, this bird sat outside Jemima's window and sang. It was the only time of the day it appeared. It was her alarm clock!
- I've never heard frogs that croaked so loud. During the rainy season, they croak all the time, especially at night
- The rainy season cools the air down to twenty-one to twenty-five Celsius at night
- Nothing happens fast—or on time! We made six trips to the Land Registry office regarding property to build a church
- There is construction everywhere!
- Pepto Bismol and Imodium can be your best friends
- Driving at night is really disconcerting. Many people, especially taxi drivers, drive with their headlights off until meeting a car and then they flash them on
- My ankles are permanently swollen

Interesting Events

- The clinics at Community Nine Church and Ashalley-Botwe church (described in Chapter Two)
- Traveling to Cape Coast and Elmina, staying at the Elmina Hotel, visiting the Slave Castle at Elmina
- Sitting on a rock in a tidal pool when a large wave came in off the ocean and swept me right off the rock and into the water. Everyone had a great laugh!
- Meeting a woman, Mary Appiah, who attended Aldersgate College in Moosejaw, Saskatchewan, and knew my Aunt Marion and Uncle Bill Rodberg

- Meeting the First Lady of Ghana, the President's wife, Mrs. Nana Konadu Agyeman Rawlings, in her office. She was a classmate of Jemima's

- Two meetings with the *Project Reach Out Ghana* board

It was a terrific experience, but I was ready to go home. We had a tearful goodbye at the airport. At Customs they x-rayed my bags and accused me of taking their "antiquities" out of the country. I couldn't see how that was possible as all the wood that I bought was purchased at the Arts Center (their craft market), but they insisted that I had to pay a "Museum Tax" of fifty dollars U.S. I was anxious to get out of Ghana without ending up in custody, so I paid that tax—plus another unofficial tax—at two stops on the way to the departure lounge after going through Customs. They said I wasn't allowed to take any Ghanaian money out of the country, so I had to give them the few cedis (their currency) I had hoped to keep as souvenirs. Finally, we boarded and took off for Amsterdam.

Project Reach Out Ghana board

On the trip home I determined that my report to *Project Reach Out Canada* would include my belief that God was calling me to return to Ghana yearly, if possible, and to take teams of volunteers every two years to help in the ministry in Ghana.

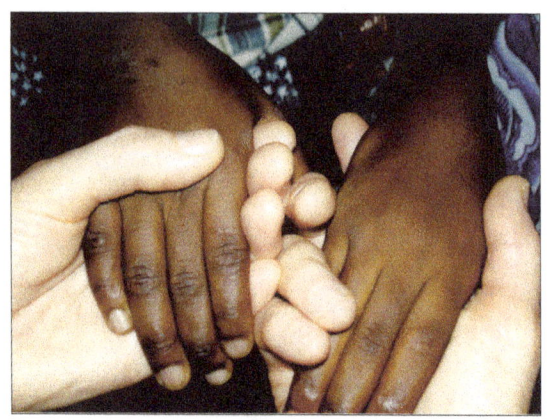

Helping Hands

"A way for Canadian Christians to show God's love to the people of Ghana by meeting physical needs, especially those of women and children."

From the constitution of Project Reach Out

Chapter 2

First Ghana Clinic
Thursday, May 27, 1993

We held our first *Project Reach Out* clinic in Ghana in the Community Nine Church and hoped everything was in place. Although we had held a short planning meeting a few days earlier, trying to anticipate every need, we had to send someone by bus to pick up the last of the medications we needed. We decided to have a registration table where we recorded everyone's name and address so that people who came to the clinic could be contacted later by the church. Each person was given a piece of paper showing their name, sex, and age. This went with them to the assessment table where temperatures and blood pressures were taken and initial assessments were done. Next came the visit with the doctor. Where necessary, he would write a diagnosis and a prescription on the paper which would then be taken to the medication table to be filled. The medication table was manned by Selena Arthur, a nurse and the wife of Rev. Mike Arthur, a *Project Reach Out Ghana (PROG)* board member.

Two hundred and eighty people registered! Unbelievable! The men often tried to get ahead in the line, despite our efforts at organization. There were lots of crying babies, but generally, people were patient. Jemima interpreted for me while I did assessments.

Although we were scheduled to close the clinic at six p.m., mothers were desperate for their sick babies to be cared for, so we continued until eight p.m. Dr. Arthur, a *PROG* board member, had to go to his job at the hospital at 6:45, but we continued seeing people. There was no electricity so Joe pulled the car around to an open door and shone the headlights in so we could see the temperatures on the thermometer and read the registration slips. Only one in eight people, even young people, had normal blood pressure; some were very high. There were many sick children—malaria, infections, sore eyes, diarrhea, and vomiting. Not enough hands to do everything, and my ears hurt from the stethoscope. We ended up having people come back the next day from ten to twelve thirty p.m. Thirty-five people were seen the following day.

Two newspaper reporters came and took pictures. Dr. Arthur heard on the radio a report of the clinic, but it was almost two weeks before an article with pictures appeared in the newspaper. As a result of the report that we had no electricity for the clinic, the utilities company put up poles and an electrician hooked up the fuses, so there was electricity in the church!

With such a good response, we decided to do a clinic at the new Ashalley-Botwe Church. On Saturday June fifth, Dr. Arthur and I went work at the clinic. More than one hundred and fifty people came. At ten-thirty, four public health nurses arrived to do an immunization clinic where they immunized eighty small children. They told Dr. Arthur that they always had trouble getting people to show up for their immunization clinics in Ashalley-Botwe, but because it was the church that was sponsoring the clinic, people brought their children. At this time, there was no health care scheme in Ghana so people had to pay for all their care but the church clinics gave free medical care.

At this clinic, we realized that the people were much younger than in Tema. Very few people over the age of fifty, and many more pregnant women and several newborns arrived for care. Almost everyone had hypertension, and many had open sores. The children were generally undersized for their age and many had bloated stomachs from malnutrition or worms. Many needed dental care. We gave out toothbrushes and toothpaste that had been donated by Dr. Weatherhead, a dentist from our church in Brockville. The clinic lasted two-and-one-half hours longer than was advertised, but we managed to see everyone.

Dr. Arthur, myself and Jemima Ocran at Ashalley-Botwe Church

The following day, June sixth, was the official opening of the Ashalley-Botwe church. It took several vehicles to take everyone from Community Nine Church in Tema who wanted to go to the Ashalley-Botwee church opening. I ended up in the front seat of an eleven seat van carrying thirty-five people! We squeezed in with seven people in the front seat!

Dr. Darco, a friend of Joe and Jemima, and his friend Dr. Bimpong, had started a clinic. I was able to visit this very busy clinic on the second floor of a large building in Ashiaman. They were trying to build their own clinic and had applied for a loan from the bank. It had been over two years since the application and still no loan. The bank was charging thirty-seven percent interest for the loan!

Medical care in a developing country certainly has its challenges!

Chapter 3

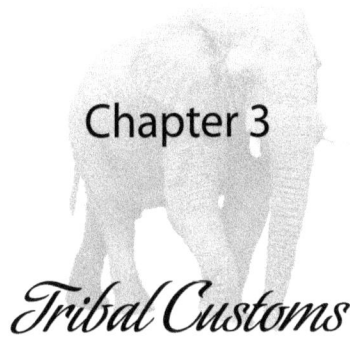

Tribal Customs

Every country has its particular customs. To us, the customs of other countries seem strange.

Akwaaba–Welcome

When you are invited to someone's home in Ghana, arriving at the appointed time is not necessarily expected. Then there is a proper way of greeting someone. When they come to the door you stay seated; the guest comes into your home and says hello, then removes his or her shoes and then shakes your hand. They then greet everyone present with a handshake and a hello, from right to left around the room. Then the guest sits and no one says anything until he or she has been served a glass of water and drinks it all. Then the host rises and shakes everyone's hand again and welcomes each person. After the host is seated again, he asks, "Why have you come?"—even if you have been invited by the host. After this, conversation can start.

The Queen Mother

The queen mother chooses the king from her family. This is where the term "matriarchal culture" originates. In Joe's family, his grandmother was the queen mother of his tribe. Her daughter's sons were eligible to be king. Joe's name is Ocran, but to his tribe he is known as the son of his mother, not his father. If he was chosen to be king, he could keep his name for personal use but would be given a traditional family name to use in his official capacity.

Funerals

A funeral is an important occasion in the life of a family. It takes a long time to let everyone know that someone has died, so the body is kept in a refrigerator or freezer at the mortuary for up to a month or more. There is a daily rental fee for the mortuary. Usually, a family meeting takes place at the end of the first week after the death. This is a meeting to make plans for how to let people know about the death, set the date of the funeral, plan for the service, plan the after-party, and plan the housing and feeding of people.

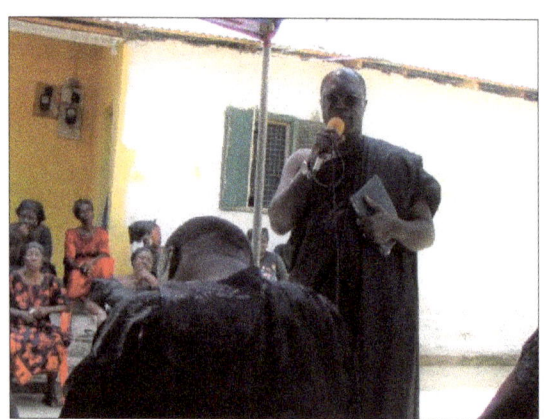
Joe speaking at Jemima's mother's funeral family planning meeting

The clothes one wears to a funeral are important. Men usually wear the traditional twelve-yard piece of black cloth wrapped around the body and over the shoulder. The women wear red and black fabric if the person that has died is under seventy years of age and white and black if the person is over seventy.

The family all wears black, not only for the funeral, but for a year or so afterward.

The actual funeral celebration starts on Friday night of the appointed weekend. The body is brought home from the mortuary, dressed, and put in a bed where it lies in state in the home. Friends come and keep vigil all night. There is much crying. Saturday morning, the body is put in a casket and taken to the church. The funeral service includes eulogies, and usually features family members speaking, preaching, and singing. A special booklet containing the life history and accomplishments of the deceased in articles, stories, and pictures contributed by friends, is given to each person present. Special souvenirs such as coffee mugs, handkerchiefs or pens with the name, birth date, date of death, and picture of the deceased are given as well.

Following the burial, everyone returns to the family's home for refreshments. Often whole streets are blocked off for a noisy party with lots of eating, drinking, and dancing that may last all night. Each person who attends the wake or funeral is expected to pay money to the family to help defray the funeral expenses. Usually, the amount each person has donated is announced on the loudspeaker. On Sunday the family again assembles at the church for both a morning service and an afternoon service, to thank everyone who took part in

Fantasy coffins for sale

the funeral. Then there is another preaching session. A funeral is a very expensive undertaking, especially if the deceased is the mother of the family. It can often bankrupt a family. On the first anniversary of the death, the whole family gets together for another wake. On the Saturday there is crying and the remembering of stories, with another church service on Sunday.

If a family can afford it, they can have a "fantasy" coffin made. These can be in any shape; for example, a fish, a chicken, a rocket ship, or a bottle of Coke.

Outdooring

When a new baby is born all the friends, relatives and neighbours come to the house, and the father announces that the baby has been born. There is much clapping, cheering and yelling. The one I experienced happened across the street at seven a.m. Tradition says the baby must stay indoors for seven days and must not be named until the eighth day. In former times, when the mortality rate for newborns was very high, they reasoned that if the baby lived until the eighth day it would be considered a human being and therefore needed a name. The waiting period was to lessen the pain that the mother would go through, should the baby die before the eighth day. The elders believe it is more painful to lose a *named* baby before the eighth day. On the naming day, there is a big party with food and drinks, and the father's family arrives to name the baby.

Engagement and Marriage

The tribal marriage is a contract between families. The families get together and sign a contract, seal it with a drink and the couple become either engaged or married. Neither the bride nor the groom needs to be present. The engagement party that I attended was a Christian ceremony. The bride was the daughter of Rev. Mike and Selena Arthur, and the groom was a Free Methodist Minister. The families were present, and the groom's godmother spoke for the groom's family. She brought gifts for the bride's father and mother. The bride's oldest brother was given money as a thank you for taking such good care of his sister. The groom's family presented a suitcase of clothes for the bride and an engagement ring. There was plenty of food and drink and much laughter. After several attempts by the bride's brother to trick the groom's family into accepting a substitute for the bride, the real bride was presented to them. The groom was not present. He came just as the party was ending. The actual church wedding took place the following day.

In some families, this tribal wedding represents the actual marriage of the couple. The bride often goes to live in the groom's family compound. If either family becomes unhappy with the union, the members can request a meeting of both families. The gifts can be returned, a divorce contract can be signed, and the marriage can be dissolved. Neither the husband nor wife needs to be present. On the other hand, if the couple is married in a church, or 'white' wedding, and the vows are officiated by a minister, the marriage is legal and binding, and the families cannot dissolve it. Some families have both a tribal and a church ceremony. Some tribal ceremonies are not registered with the government, so there is no legal record of the marriage; but the minister of a church wedding registers it, and so it is considered legal for census purposes.

Chapter 4

Known by Your Name

They say that the most important thing to a person is their name. In Ghana, frequently children are given a "day-name," which corresponds to the day in the week they were born. These day names have further meanings concerning the soul and character of the person. Middle names have considerably more variety and can refer to birth order, twin status, or an ancestor's middle name. Most Ghanaians have at least one name from this system. Many families give a child a "Christian" name, then a day-name and sometimes another family name plus the father's surname.

Below is a list of the day-names used by different tribes in Ghana.

Male

- Sunday: Akwasi, Kwasi, Kwesi, Akwesi, Sisi, Kacely, Kosi
- Monday: Kojo, Kwadwo, Jojo, Joojo, Kujoe
- Tuesday: Kwabena, Kobe, Kobi, Ebo, Kabelah, Komla, Kwabela, Kobby
- Wednesday: Kwaku, Abeiku, Kuuku, Kweku
- Thursday: Yaw, Ekow, Yao

- Friday: Kofi, Fifi, Fiifi, Yoofi
- Saturday: Kwame, Kwamena, Kwamina

Female

- Sunday: Akosua, Akasi, Akos, Esi, Awesi
- Monday: Adwoa, Adjoa, Adzoa, Adwoma
- Tuesday: Abena, Araba, Abenayo
- Wednesday: Akua, Aku, Kukua, Akuma
- Thursday: Aba, Yaa, Yawa, Baaba, Awo
- Friday: Afua, Afia, Afi
- Saturday: Ama

Some Examples:

Kofi Annan, the chairman of the United Nations for many years, was a Friday-born male.

Joseph Yaw Ocran, the founder of *Project Reach Out* and the founder of the Wesleyan Church in Ghana is a Thursday-born male.

If I had been born in Ghana, my name would have been Carole Abena Brown Tanney, and my husband's surname "Tanney" might not have been included.

I have met many people with names that would be unusual to Western culture. Here are a few: Comfort, Destiny, Virtue, Peace, Precious, Famous, Divine, Mercy, Blessing, Favour, Happiness, Princess, Queen, Charity, Love, Success, God's Testimony, Thank God, Wisdom, Wonder, and Gifty.

Chapter 5

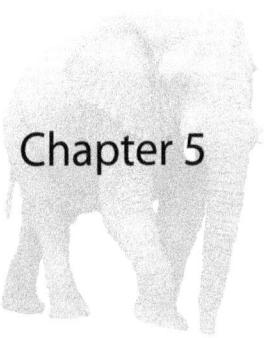

Customs Experiences

I've made it a policy to always be honest and direct with Customs when entering a country and never to offer any information that is not an answer to a direct question. Over the years, I've transported many different things through Customs into countries. When I first started going to Ghana, I knew there were many things Jemima dearly loved but could not get in Ghana. One of those things was broccoli. Several times I wrapped up fresh broccoli and packed it in my carry-on luggage as a special treat for her. One trip I took a head of fresh celery. Another trip I took a pound of bacon.

If you have ever had the privilege of eating Ghanaian pineapple, especially Cape Coast pineapple you will know what I'm talking about when I say I have never tasted anything so good. So I thought it would be a nice treat to take some home. On the way to the airport to leave Ghana, we stopped and bought seven pineapples.

I wrapped them in plastic bags (in Ghana they call them rubber bags) and put them in my checked luggage. In those days it was possible to carry fruit into the country. We had previously brought pineapple through customs from Hawaii. When I collected my luggage in Toronto, I could smell pineapple! One of the questions on the Customs form is, "Do you have any fruit?" I answered yes, but I didn't put down seven pineapples. When the Customs officer asked me about the pineapple—of course he could smell it and it smelled so good—he asked me how many I had. I told him seven. He smiled and said, "You can have two. Just leave the other five right here with me!" I laughed and said he must have been a Ghanaian Customs officer. (In those days it was common knowledge that if a Customs officer in Ghana wanted something in your luggage, he or she just helped themselves.) He laughed and let me go through. When I got home and unpacked, one pineapple had exploded and was mush, but the other six made good gifts for my family and friends. My suitcase was permanently stained from the pineapple juice.

Another year, someone had asked me to bring home a garden machete for him. He had seen one that someone else brought back from Ghana and wanted one for himself. These implements are not like regular machetes but have a hook at the end of the blade that sticks in the ground. You turn it to pull out weeds. I thought perhaps if someone wanted one, then others could want them when they saw them, so I bought six, hoping to sell them at our Ghana Market.

The Customs form asks: "Do you have any tools?" I checked "yes." The Customs officer asked me what kind of tools I had and I replied, "Garden machetes." He told me I couldn't bring weapons into the country. Of course I said they were not weapons but a special kind of garden implement. He let me pass without confiscating them but commented, "A tool to some and a weapon to others."

When entering Ghana, like in any country, Customs agents always ask why you have come and what you are bringing into the country. I usually say, "I'm bringing gifts for friends, and school supplies to help with the ministry of Rev. Joe Ocran." They say, "Oh Pastor Joe," and let me pass without opening bags. Only once during an early trip were my bags opened, and one of the dentists had one of her bags opened when arriving for the first dental clinic.

However, leaving the country, there seems to be more vigilance. Before sophisticated x-ray equipment, the agents always opened my bags when I was leaving the country. When leaving with the second dental team in 2007, they asked what we had. As they were starting to open the bags, I asked them if they had seen the television news the night before where our team was featured doing free dental clinics in Northern Ghana. They closed the bags, saying "Thank you for helping our people." They put check marks on the bags of everyone in the team and put our luggage through unopened. The only items we had in our luggage were the things we were going to sell in Canada in the Ghana Market, and we had permission to be exempt from duty. Lawrence Reimer had purchased the head of an ox which he had dried and wrapped securely in his luggage, but they did not even ask about that! It was to be partnered with a deer head in his garage at home.

Chapter 6

1994 Trip

Rev. Conley surveying the Church building site with the Ocrans

Rev. Earl Conley was traveling to visit the mission in November 1994. Jemima had been sick and was recovering from surgery, so I went along with Rev. Conley to help Jemima and to visit the work of *Project Reach Out Ghana*. The trip was for only fifteen days.

The very first night when we were at the mission home in Tema, someone stole the brand new ten-speed bicycle that Albert had just received —even though it was in the locked compound. He had forgotten to lock it in the storage room before he went to bed.

There had been a death in Jemima's family, and she went

Pastors training class with Rev. Conley

to be with her family for the Friday night wake.

With only fifteen days for this trip, we started working as soon as we arrived. It was a rush to get all the medications that we needed for medical clinics, but we were ready to head out to Ashiaman on Saturday, November twenty-sixth, for a clinic to start at ten a.m. We worked steadily until four p.m. Rev. Conley preached at every opportunity. He also did a pastor's training session.

Carole doing the medical clinic at Ashiaman

This time of year is the start of the Harmattan, a season in the West African subcontinent, which occurs from the end of November to the middle of March. It is characterized by the dry and dusty northeasterly trade wind of the same name which blows from the Sahara Desert over West Africa into the Gulf of Guinea. Jemima's asthma is greatly affected by the dust, and she has difficulty breathing.

On a trip to Sogakope, we were stopped by the police for speeding. Joe paid the fine on the roadside, and when we got home, he found that his wallet was missing. It contained not only U.S. cash but all his papers for living in Ghana, the children's Canadian birth certificates, and visas. Jemima disappeared to her prayer closet, and we all had a very intense time of prayer. At six p.m., the police called to say they had found Joe's wallet at the police check-point. The police chief arrived with the wallet, and everything was in it. What a miracle! At that time in Ghana, the police were known for corruption, and so to have all the money, as well as the papers, returned was truly a miracle.

Joe and Rev. Conley drove to Ekroful and Empiro in the Central region to meet with people and to hold services. While there, they were given a goat as a gift. When they returned the next day the goat accompanied them, but it had to travel in the air-conditioned car with them, and it appeared that the goat caught a cold. It coughed all night and kept everyone awake. Jemima found it a good home quickly.

On December fourth, we all traveled to Asite, a small village near Somanga, about one-and-a-half hours away from Tema. Rev. Conley preached under a big mango tree in the centre of the village. Thirty-five people stood and prayed to accept Christ during the service. Following the service, we set up a medical clinic. Rev. Mike Arthur, a *Project Reach Out Ghana* board member, interpreted for me. We saw two hundred and five people. It was at this clinic that the fire ants attacked and bit my legs. Very painful!

The chief had donated a piece of property for the building of a church. Several years after the church was built, the pastor found people cutting down the palm trees on the property. Palm trees are used to make palm wine, which is a very sought after drink. When he approached the chief asking why they were doing this on the church's property, the chief said that he donated the property but not the trees!

During this visit, it seemed that there was a large number of people coming to the mission home, all wanting something. Money flows from Jemima's purse. She has a huge purse that is always open!

God worked in people's hearts on this trip with Rev. Conley preaching God's Word, and many people were helped in the medical clinics.

Chapter 7

The First Team – 1995
This Little Light of Mine

1995 was an exciting year. In 1993, when I made my first trip to Ghana by myself, I decided to travel to Ghana every year and take a group of volunteers every two years. God directed me to take my first team to Ghana in 1995. The team consisted of seven people: Lawrence Eyre, a farmer; his wife Thelma, a church librarian; Rayleen Hobbs, a retired nurse; Sherrie Rounding Davis, a former pastor's wife and all-round "jack of all trades"; David Dewick, a truck driver; Joan Barrance, a retired teacher and me, a nurse. I had been on several tours before where I was one of the tour participants and one trip where I was assisting my dad in helping with the tour group logistics. I had never led a team before and didn't really know what the leader was supposed to do.

The team really consisted of two groups: one group of four that would stay for two weeks, and another group of three that would stay four weeks. It is a challenge to find meaningful volunteer work for everyone in their field of expertise. Joe and Jemima found a four-bedroom house for us to rent in Achimota, a suburb of Accra, more than an hour away from the home where Joe and Jemima lived in Tema.

It was a long trip, taking the airport bus from Kingston at noon, leaving Canada from Toronto about six-thirty p.m., a seven and a half hour flight to Amsterdam, an eight-hour stopover in Amsterdam and then another seven-hour flight to Accra, the capital of Ghana arriving about eight p.m. After going through Customs with twenty-two large pieces of luggage plus our carry-ons, we were finally on the road in the dark. Joe and Jemima were there to meet us and drove us over terrible roads to our accommodation. There were huge pot-holes in the road that the driver had to negotiate around. Two famous remarks were made on this trip. One from the first trip to the guest house was made by Lawrence Eyre: "We're never going to make it!" On many other trips where the roads were bad, that phrase was used to the amusement of many people. The second remark was from Sherrie Rounding Davis; it was "Oh my!" Her response to everything she saw was, "Oh my."

Having had no experience with team travel, dealing with finances was a challenge. We decided we would have a "kitty" to pay expenses. Everyone would donate one hundred dollars U.S. to the kitty at the start of the trip, and I would pay for all the expenses until the money ran out, then each person would donate more money. This worked well for the next ten years - until I took an accountant who wanted everything paid for before we left Canada, with the corresponding receipts for income tax for all

Lawrence and Dave with the local painters in Asite

expenses, not just the air flight- a nightmare for me trying to estimate expenses for the whole trip before we got to Ghana where the prices of things change every day.

There are always unexpected conflicts with a group of people who had never traveled together before - what to wear to the market, how to divide up the housekeeping duties, personality conflicts, who would sit in the front and so on.

There was no conflict on the jobs each would do, however. Lawrence and Dave fixed things around the mission home and were taken on two trips to Asite where a new church had just been built. They painted the building with the help of the local people.

The Tema clinic

Rayleen and Carole, being nurses, ran a day clinic in the Community Nine church building with Dr. Joseph Arthur, one of the *Ghana Project Reach Out* board members, and Selena Arthur, the wife of another board member. One child who was brought to the clinic had a temperature of over one hundred four degrees Fahrenheit. She was admitted to the hospital with infectious hepatitis. Three of her siblings were also treated. Dr. Arthur said she would have died without treatment.

Clinics were also held in Duakwa and Anum. Everyone is drawn to a clinic to see the strange white people and to get something free. We had brought toothbrushes and toothpaste from Canada. It was difficult to determine a way to demonstrate how to clean one's teeth properly. A denturist in Brockville donated a pair of dentures. At the Anum clinic, it was decided that Sherrie and Dave would give out toothbrushes and demonstrate their use.

During the church service it had rained, and the rivulets of water were running through the bamboo and thatch building where the service was held. After the service, we held the clinic in the building, and Sherrie and Dave went outside to give out the toothbrushes to the children. Every child in the town arrived, pushing and crowding each other in the mud, trying to get a free toothbrush. There was no point trying to show them how to clean their teeth. Dave and Sherrie had a terrible time trying not to get crushed. Finally, they ended up sitting on the tailgate of the bus teaching choruses and songs to the children while the rest of us saw one hundred twenty-five adults and as many children at the clinic. Jemima joined Sherrie and Dave and had a Sunday School service, and invited them all back every Sunday for Sunday School.

Thelma and Joan helped at clinics, but their job was to sort books that had been previously shipped and organize them onto library shelves. There were reference books for pastors, children's books, and fiction/biography books for adults. The concept of a lending library was not common in Ghana at that time. Once the people had a book in hand, it was often considered "theirs."

Jemima owned a shop where she sold cake decorating and wedding catering supplies, and she wanted to learn how to decorate wedding cakes. Sherrie is a cake decorator, so she held cake decorating classes for several ladies to learn the basics.

At the end of two weeks, four of the team left to travel back to Canada. Sherrie, Joan, and I remained in Ghana. Joan was the president of the Anglican Women's Organization in Eastern Ontario, and she had met the Bishop of Kumasi on one of his trips to Canada. She was invited to visit him and his wife at their home in Kumasi. At the end of her two-week stay, Joe and I drove to pick her up. We were invited to the Kumasi cathedral for a women's conference. Everyone attending had to wear white so the Bishop's wife found dresses for Joan and me to wear.

The cathedral is a massive building, and hundreds of people attended the lively service. I don't remember the topics discussed or anything about the service except that in the middle of it, the power went off. It was very dark in this huge building; we couldn't see anything! I remembered that I had a small flashlight on my key chain, so I got it out and turned it on. It was the only light in the entire building. Everyone was straining to see who had the "torch," making me the "hit" of the service. Everyone wanted to shake hands with the obroni (white person) with the light.

This turned out to be a good object lesson: one little light plus one person doing what they can, can be the light in the darkness for someone who needs a light. God has called each of us to be light to others and people will want to be near those who offer light in their world.

I learned an important lesson on this trip that has served me well over the years. The Bishop's wife was an army nurse. I commented that I wished I had brought some of the medicines left over from our clinics to give her. She asked me what medicines I had. When I told her Tylenol and ASA plus a few other things, she said, "We don't need those medicines. We have the fever tree." The Neem tree has leaves that contain acetylsalicylic acid (ASA). When brewed with hot water and given as a drink, the tea will reduce a fever. Treatments we use in the West and regard as superior, are not necessarily needed by people in other countries. They often have effective treatments for common diseases of their own cultures.

Reflections from Sherrie Davis

"My first trip to Ghana in 1995 was quite a culture shock to me. It was breathtaking to see the market, the ocean, and the countryside, but most of all the people.

Sherrie with Ghanaian children

"The women of Ghana reminded me of Proverbs Thirty-One and verse twenty-seven: "She watches over the affairs of her household and does not eat the fruit of idleness." They were beautifully dressed in the bright colours of their country. I have never seen such hard working women, beautifully dressed in the bright colours of their culture, with children on their backs, eggs, wood, or charcoal on their heads, or other items they could sell or use in their homes.

"When we arrived at Sakumono church, the people were already praising, singing and dancing to honour our Lord and Saviour. It was not as if they were waiting for God, but as though God was right there at that very moment, and so He was!

"I learned from watching people: they had joy, peace and love for our Lord. So Matthew nineteen, verse twenty-six is true: even when we have little, 'With God everything is possible.'

"The children were amazing. They played with anything they could find or make. They swam in the same water the cattle drank. The women used the same water for their laundry and drinking. We found the critical need for clean water and drilled wells in every village.

"Leaving Ghana, as we hugged and said goodbye, I knew that my real journey had just begun because God had opened my heart to be committed to the work in Ghana. Both my husband, Brian, and I have returned to Ghana several times. We have had the great joy of hosting Rev. Joe Ocran and his family in our home when they come to Canada. It was an awakening to my soul and a privilege to be part of this mission."

Chapter 8

1996 Luggage Problem?

On February fifteenth, 1996, Laurence Croswell and I headed to Ghana. I took the airport bus from Kingston again this year, but I left my carry on luggage on the bus. Panic time! The bus was scheduled to stop at the Carlingview Motel, so I called them, and they got the luggage off the bus and brought it to the airport for me. If I ever need a place to stay in Toronto, it will be the Carlingview Motel!

At the airport check-in desk, one bag was overweight. The airline had instituted a thirty-two kilogram weight regulation since our last trip, so I had to unpack the bag and take out enough weight to meet the thirty-two-kilogram/fifty-pound limit. We had to take out two cartons of toothbrushes and toothpaste. The check-in attendant suggested we should wrap it up in plastic and put it through as luggage, which we did without charge, thanks to KLM. Unfortunately, when we retrieved our luggage in Accra, it was not there; someone must have liked the package and it was gone.

Before we arrived, Jemima had been trying to find a piano teacher for Diella; two weeks later, a woman came to the house to ask about the lessons. She said that she worked for KLM and had a package at the lost and found with my name on it. The next day she brought the package with the toothbrushes and toothpaste to the house. Apparently, God even cares about toothpaste!

We had still more luggage problems. The strap on our duffel bag was broken, so it had to go to be repaired. We didn't get it back until shortly before we had to take the luggage to the airport to leave; however, we managed to have it packed and ready to go on time!

When I took the first team in 1995, we decided to take them into the city of Amsterdam for a tour. It was so successful that Laurence and I decided to do the same. The Canal tours were not running because of the cold, so we booked a bus tour around the city and surrounding area. We made it back to the airport just in time to board the plane for Accra.

Laurence and Joe held a four-day training session for pastors. Since they were gone all day, Jemima and I shopped for groceries, some Ghana Market items, and I helped out at her shop. We made plans for clinics and bought medicines for them. The water was off every day on rotating times, some days throughout the day and the next day all night. It was a task trying to do laundry, water all Jemima's plants and have showers while there was water available. I've since learned to have "bucket showers." It was so hot at this time of year that I have decided that I will never go to Ghana in February again! Because of the heat and drought, there was a shortage of water coming over the Akosombo Dam, so the water company instituted a rationing system. Water and electricity are shut off at different times in different areas of the country.

Sunday we drove to Otrokpe church where Laurence preached, and we held a clinic in the afternoon. One hundred and seven people registered plus some babies. There were no older people but lots of children. However, we encountered no serious illnesses.

I had met Dr. Darko on a previous visit to Ghana. He and his partner, Dr. Bempong, started a private clinic called the Darbem Clinic. I worked there for a day; it was very interesting and very hot. I helped with ten admissions, gave some medications and injections, applied some dressings, helped in the pharmacy, and started an IV. Working in the heat was tiring.

Jemima picked branches and palm nuts from her palm tree. She showed us how to strip the palm branches and make brooms to sweep the compound and how to pick the fruit to make palm oil. However, one thing I have never been able to develop a taste for is palm oil soup.

Laurence was writing a book, and he wrote several chapters while sitting under the shade of the palm tree. We had a surprise party for his birthday with a musical candle that we couldn't shut off even by putting it in a glass of water! Albert and Diella had a great laugh over that.

On Thursday, February twenty-seventh, we held a clinic at the Sakumono church. The Department of Health visited and informed us that we had to make people pay for treatment. The government clinics charge people for care, and we were taking away their business. We couldn't set a fee so we put a plate on the medication table and told people to "donate" whatever they could afford for their treatment.

Sunday, March third, we headed for the city of Ho. It is almost at the Togo border in Eastern Ghana. Laurence preached in the open under a canopy with some good-sized holes in it. After the service, we set up a clinic under the canopy and registered one hundred twenty-three people plus about ten more children. Many elderly people came to the clinic with conditions common to the elderly: hypertension, arthritic and rheumatic pain, and dental problems. A thunderstorm developed and the holes in the canopy became a big problem. We had to close the clinic in a hurry, but we were able to dispense medications from the back of the bus with the lift-up door which gave some protection from the rain. While the clinic was on, Joe took Laurence, Diella and Albert to the village of Anum to greet the pastor and the people there.

Laurence preaching at Ho

Joe and Lawrence went to Accra to look at vans that could be used as a mobile clinic vehicle. We were able to accumulate enough funds from the previous four years to buy one.

On the way back to Canada, we had a six-hour layover in the huge Amsterdam airport and met a couple from our own church in Brockville! We landed in Toronto and took the airport bus to Kingston. Because it was February and winter in Canada, I had asked my husband, Lorne, to bring my winter coat, hat and mitts and also a coat for Laurence. Laurence is not as big as my husband was, so the down-filled coat Lorne brought was much too big. However, despite the very large coat, he was shivering and so cold that he couldn't even talk. We made it safely home once again. Thank you, Lord.

Chapter 9

1997 – New Mitsubishi Van Mobile Clinic

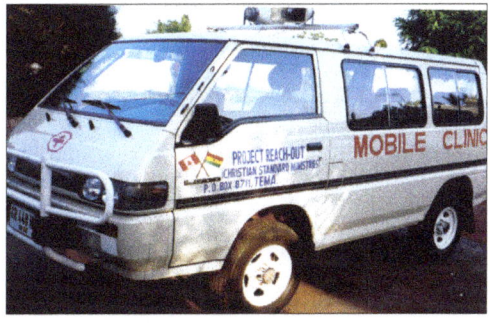

After four years of fund-raising in Canada, *Project Reach Out Ghana* was able to buy a Mitsubishi van for a mobile medical clinic. We hired a driver, a nurse and a helper to enable the mobile clinic to make a circuit every month to thirty villages. The purpose was to provide health care for approximately 10,000 people that would normally have no access to medical care.

In Ghana, getting permission and the necessary documents to do anything is a convoluted process. Getting licensing, insurance and so on from the Ministry of Health, Ministry of Transportation, and the other bureaucratic and political institutions takes a long time. Finally, in January of 1997, Ghana implemented national polio immunization, but public health nurses didn't have any way to get to the villages to immunize people. Someone suggested that maybe *Project Reach Out* would provide free transportation for the Public Health department. A temporary license was granted, and the clinic was on its way. Once the immunization campaign ended, the van was given a permanent license and the work of *Project Reach Out* began.

On July twenty-sixth, 1997, a five-member team from Canada arrived to volunteer with *Project Reach Out*. Our team consisted of me, Muriel Wolanski, a nurse, Vivian Alguire, a home care worker, Hazel, a teacher, and Harold, a carpenter. Our first mobile clinic visit was on July twenty-eighth, to the village of Kpone-Bawaleski accompanied by clinic nurse Margaret, a helper Apalonia, a hospital nurse Felicia and the driver. We treated one hundred people at tables set up under a tree in the village, a tiring but fulfilling day. During this trip, Vivian and Hazel sorted books that had been previously shipped and Harold did carpentry work at the new Sakumono Church. On July twenty-ninth, Muriel and I headed off with the clinic staff and a public health nurse to the village of Gbetsile. In each village, we drove the van around with the loudspeaker announcing that a clinic was to be held. There was no previous planning with the village elders but one hundred

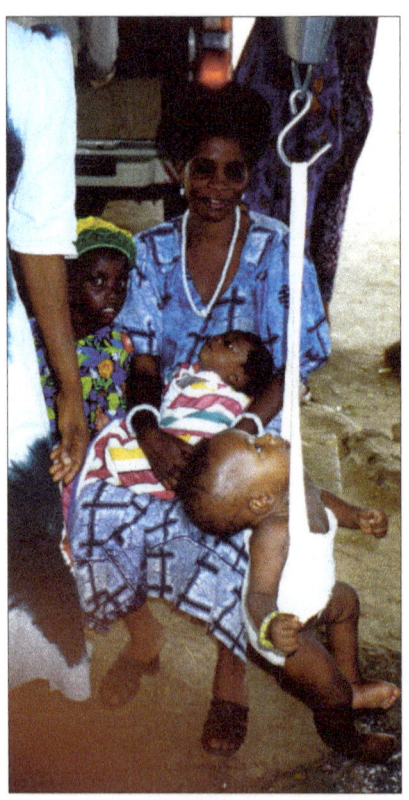

Baby being weighed in a tree

thirty-four people registered and received care. The public health nurse immunized babies and taught mothers of newborns about infant care. They set up a primitive, but effective scale to weigh the babies by attaching a scale to a harness, hanging the contraption from a tree limb and putting the baby in the harness!

1997 Team

Harold encountered a problem. Ghanaians typically hold hand-saws with the blade facing away from them and saw away from themselves. In Canada, carpenters use saws with the blades facing them and saw towards themselves. The Ghanaian carpenter who Harold was working with, wouldn't work with him unless he sawed the Ghanaian way; Harold wouldn't do it any other way than what he was used to in Canada. Stalemate! It has been our policy that we don't go into Ghana and tell them how to do things our way. We go with the Ghanaians in charge and do what they tell us to do unless it puts us in an unsafe position. The following day, Harold went back to the church to finish the door frames, but the Ghanaian carpenter was not there. To add to Harold's frustrations, when he went to the

Harold sawing the "Ghanaian" way (backwards)

55

church site a couple of days later, he discovered that someone had broken in and stolen the window and door frames he had made—so he had to start all over again. He was very discouraged and wondered if his experience in Ghana was worth it.

On August first we headed for Otrokpe. Pastor Joseph Narh gave us a tour of his agricultural project and then a demonstration of his women's literacy class. He also had organized a medical clinic for later in the day. We saw eighty-eight people that afternoon and provided plenty of first aid. One thing we encountered that we had not discussed before was the many people who needed glasses.

Sunday, August third we drove for three hours to the village of Atuakrom. Joe preached, and after lunch, we set up for a clinic that saw over one hundred people presenting with serious skin conditions, high blood pressure, goiters, and diabetes as well as many sick children. Some conditions we were not equipped to treat. Hazel, Vivian, and Harold worked with over two hundred children singing choruses, playing games and having races.

On August fourth we went back to Kpone-Bawaleshi with the clinic van. It was an unorganized clinic, so we weren't able to

Village clinic with mobile clinic van

count the number of people we saw but thirty babies were immunized against yellow fever. The chief asked me to see a villager who couldn't come to the clinic. Muriel, our clinic nurse and I headed off to a hut, and there I saw the only case of leprosy I ever saw in Ghana.

On August fifth, the mobile clinic arrived late, and we headed for the Ashiaman Barrier where we saw thirty people; the public health nurse gave only ten immunizations. After we got back to the house, we worked for two-and-a-half hours updating clinic records. Harold stayed behind to help build a laundry room for Jemima.

On August sixth we went with the clinic van to the site for the Ashalley-Botwe daycare building. During this clinic, we saw and treated one hundred and sixty people, many with colds, fevers, high blood pressure, malaria, and worms. By the end of it, we were all very tired.

However, it wasn't all work and no play for this trip. We took several short trips to craft markets to shop, and we spent two days traveling to Kumasi where we visited the cultural centre and did some shopping. The power was off, but we were still able to get a meal and have a good sleep. The following day we drove on to Obuasi, Joe's home town and then to his sister's village. We visited Cape Coast, toured Elmina castle where slaves were held before being sent to the New World on slave ships, and then drove back to Accra. It was a long and tiring trip of three hundred forty kilometres the first day and four hundred forty kilometres the second day. When you say you travelled four hundred forty-six kilometres in Canada, no one thinks much of it, but in Ghana over rutted roads, in terrible traffic jams, through ever-present road construction sites, it is an extremely tiring trip.

On August tenth we went to Ashalley-Botwe to church with pastor Lawrence Yaboa preaching. They had several offerings. This church had a fund-raising project using the day of the week you were born. They took up an offering featuring each day of the week; people born on that day contributed their offering and counted to see which day raised the most money. Thursday won! Following those seven offerings, there was a tithe offering followed by a regular offering. Of course, with the obronis (white people) present they expected the offerings to be higher. After the church service, we held another clinic. Ninety-two people had registered, but a few extras worked their way in. Many of the people needed to see a dentist.

We held eight clinics on this trip, more than any other team trip I have taken. We treated between six hundred and seven hundred people. Having the mobile clinic certainly made a huge difference.

Muriel Wolanski enjoyed the experience and giving medical care to those in need so much that when she went home, she went on several other missions trips with her home church in Hamilton. Thank you, Lord, for another productive trip with You watching over us and keeping us safe.

Reflections From Vivian Algurie,
Team Member of the 1997 Team

"My trip to Ghana in 1997 was a memorable experience. It was encouraging to see where *Project Reach Out* funds were helping the people of Ghana with schools, the clinic, and the farm. Traveling to the outlying villages doing medical clinics and going to churches was a joy. One thing that I remember vividly was how they openly worship our Lord and Saviour, Jesus Christ.

"Taking up their offering was quite different from Canadian churches, as they waved handkerchiefs and danced around to present their offering at the front of the church. One offering, in particular, was memorable—a bag of crushed corn with two little chicken eggs sitting on top of the corn.

"The experiences in Ghana made me want to work harder here at home to raise money to support these projects. God has surely blessed us in our work and giving. May we be ever faithful to further His work here and in Ghana."

Irene in the blue dress and her mother Sophia in white

Chapter 10

Project Reach Out Ghana's First Scholarship Student

In the late 1990's, a young widow with two children, was told that her daughter, then aged fourteen, was extremely bright. Irene had graduated from grade nine in Junior Secondary School and her mother, Sophia Bonney, desperately wanted her daughter to continue her education. However, there was no money to pay for Senior Secondary School. In Ghana after grade nine, senior secondary schools are very expensive; many are privately run. Both government and private schools were mostly boarding schools. This changed in 2017 when the government extended government-funded education to the end of grade twelve, Senior Secondary School. However, even though schools are classed as free, there are still expenses families have to pay: uniforms, supplies, books, and other fees that many families cannot afford.

Sophia had started selling eggs and chickens after her husband was tragically killed in a traffic accident. Even though her business was growing, there was no extra money for schooling. Her request for help from Jemima Ocran resulted in the first *Project Reach Out* scholarship, which was awarded to Irene. In partnership with Irene's family, *PRO* provided the money for her room and board, and Sophia paid for Irene's tuition and other fees.

After three years, Irene graduated from Senior Secondary School with a dream to be a gynecologist. Again Sophia asked Rev. Joe for a scholarship to help with university costs. *PRO* continued to provide money for her room and board, and the family paid other expenses. After four years of university, Irene graduated with high honours. She continued her education, receiving her Masters' degree. During these years, Irene worked part-time in medical research and decided that this would be her life's work.

In 2013, at the age of twenty four, Irene was married; Rev. Ocran performed the wedding ceremony. Irene was invited to study for her Ph.D. at a university outside of Ghana with a full scholarship from another organization. Sophia's son has also graduated from university.

Irene's scholarship has become the model for all *PRO* scholarships. Because education for girls is not considered as important as a boy's education, *PRO* scholarships often go to girls in partnership with the family. The recipients are required to volunteer in some way with the church or *PRO* as a way of repaying the scholarship.

Sandra, one of our scholarship students, grew up in the Tema Community Nine church and is just graduating from university with a geological engineering degree. Sandra helps with Sunday School at the Sakumono church. Florence, another scholarship student, is studying nursing and helping in the Ashalley-Botwe church.

Nursing Scholarships

I have had an interest in developing a scholarship program

to encourage young women to go into nursing. Mabel Hewitt, a *Project Reach Out Canada* board member was also very interested in this project, and started to promote donations to this fund. When it came time to grant the scholarships and apply to nursing schools, it became apparent there were no girls who qualified for the program. Applicants had to have high marks in math and science in senior secondary school, but many girls either did not completely finish secondary school, or had been absent so many days that their marks were affected negatively. Unfortunately, girls miss a week of school every month because they can't attend when they have their monthly periods.

Reflections from Nursing Scholarship Student, Ibrahim

The first nursing scholarship student accepted by the nursing school was Ibrahim Ahamadu – then called Mohammed Ibrahim – pictured with Carole and Kathy deSouza. The program was a three-year program.

"I was born into a less than well-to-do family. My father was a peasant farmer, and my mother a housewife. Because I was the first male child, I knew there was a heavy task ahead of me, especially when they got old, so I had to strive to make my future bright. How could I do it without financial assistance from a reliable source? But when *PRO* extended their wonderful good work into my life, the tables turned for the better.

"I got connected to *PRO* after my admission into nursing training college. My parents were struggling to pay the fees during the first semester of my first year. I decided to look for sponsorship from any district in the northern region. The person I contacted at the regional health directorate called me and gave me the contact number of Rev. Ocran. I met with him in Accra, signed the sponsorship documents, and returned to school in Tamale.

"I now have a reliable job which I credit to *PRO*. I can support myself, my aged parents and my siblings. Now I have smiling parents!

"God has been teaching me to be prayerful and hopeful. He said we should seek and he shall provide. God has also been teaching me to be faithful and truthful in life.

"Great thanks to you all for the wonderful work you are doing. May the good Lord bless you all."

A recent update from Ibrahim: "I am now studying in a two-year Bachelor of Science program in Kumasi, specializing in anesthesia."

This program is not a *PRO*-sponsored scholarship.

Other Scholarships

Currently, there are several Primary and Junior Secondary School students at the Wesleyan Academy receiving assistance.

Girls often can't afford sanitary pads,

Primary school scholarships with uniforms and school supplies being presented students in the village of Bomase

and their culture does not always approve of them leaving their home during their monthly periods, so they stay home one week out of every month. This has a detrimental effect on their education. At graduation, some have been absent for so many days that their grades are adversely affected. *World Hope Canada* found a pattern to make reusable, washable sanitary pads and the idea was presented to a group of sewers at Centennial Road Church called "The Sew and Sews;" they agreed to make them for us to distribute to girls in Ghana as long as they stayed in school. We are hoping that this will positively influence girls to stay in school and to excel.

Reusable sanitary pads kits being distributed to female students at Wesleyan Academy in Anum

1999 Team: Sheldon Gilmer, Paul Noren and Carole

Chapter 11

The Trip From Hell—1999

The funding from *CIDA* (*The Canadian International Development Agency*) and *Project Reach Out Canada* partner *HelpAge Canada* had just been approved. Sheldon Gilmer was our contact as a volunteer with *HelpAge Canada*. He was instrumental in writing all the proposals and reporting to *CIDA* for all six years of the funding. Sheldon has travelled all over the world. He convinced me that it was cheaper and faster to travel to Ghana through New York by Air Afrique. Traveling through the U.S. to anywhere has never been a pleasant experience for me, but I agreed. When we got to New York from Ottawa via Boston, our luggage had to be inspected and the flight was repeatedly delayed.

Because of the delay in New York, we missed our connecting flight from Cote d'Ivoire to Ghana, and we had to take a flight with Air Ethiopia. Finally, we arrived in Ghana and had to wait for Joe and Jemima to pick us up at the airport due to changes in our arrival times.

The funding from *CIDA* provided money for North/South visits (Canada to Africa) and South/South visits (travel between African countries). *Project Reach Out Ghana* was planning to start an agroforestry project for the elderly with some of the funding from *CIDA*. There was an agroforestry expert named Paul Noren who was working as a missionary in the Central African Republic in an agroforestry project. Paul was able to travel to Ghana on this funding as a consultant to *Project Reach Out Ghana* . He had many good suggestions for our Ghana project.

After Paul left to return to DRC, Sheldon and I went with Joe to the eastern area of Ghana for a Sunday service. On the return trip, four men who asked for a ride to Tema were sitting in the rear of the vehicle. In Ghana, an SUV that has two seats is considered a six-passenger vehicle but they add seats, often wooden benches, in the rear along the side of the luggage area. These men were seated there. On the trip back to Tema, we were driving along comfortably when, all of a sudden, a wheel from another vehicle came bouncing down the road toward us. We had no idea where the wheel was going to go, but it was headed directly into our path. The men in the rear started praying loudly repeating, "Jesus, Jesus, Jesus," and Joe took evasive action. The tire bounced in front of us and right over the hood of our vehicle, landing in the ditch. After catching our breath, we realized that a trotro (a local bus/van), loaded with people, was coming towards us with the axle dragging on the pavement and sparks were flying everywhere. It was careening all over the road trying to stop. Thankfully, it finally stopped with no injuries to the people aboard, and we were able to continue on our way.

Project Reach Out Ghana had been searching for a site to build our permanent clinic. Joe and I along with Mike Arthur, a *PROG* board member who spoke the local language, went down a long road (really just a path through the fields) to a village to talk to the chief. He was very interested in talking to us, but it appeared he had imbibed a bit too much before we arrived. During the conversation, he turned to me and said, "Let's get married." I said, "I'm already married." He replied, "So am I; so what?" It wasn't long until we were on our way back down the overgrown path. It turned out that he already had several wives!

Sheldon left Ghana a couple of weeks before me. It finally came time for me to start for home. The Air Afrique flight back to New York made a stop again in Cote d'Ivoire (Ivory Coast). When we got off the plane, they demanded our passports and wouldn't give them back to us. A bus drove up, and we were told that we had to take the bus to a hotel—but no one would tell us why. There was much yelling, pounding of tables, and upset. I decided not to say anything until it was time for me to get on the bus, at which time, I demanded my passport back. They would not give it to me. With no other option available, I headed to a hotel where they said we would be given a meal and a room for the night. The meal was just a very unappealing snack, served in an outdoor seating area next to an open sewer. Needless to say, I didn't eat. When I asked for a drink, they said the drink was not part of the meal. I called the manager and got my drink without having to pay for it. In fact ,I had spent my U.S. money and only had Canadian money left—and of course they wouldn't take it. To make matters worse, I was unable to do laundry before I left Ghana. This meant I had no clean underwear. I washed it out before I went to bed, but when I got up a few short hours later it was not dry, and I had to wear it wet. I remembered my grandmother's sage advice to never go out without clean underwear; however, she never said anything about wet underwear!

There was very little sleep that night. When we were brought back to the airport the next morning, everybody's passport was there but mine. The plane was boarding and still no passport. I was finally told that I had to go to the police station to try to get my passport back. It was a very trying time. I found out later from a woman in Brockville (who was married to a man from Cote d'Ivoire) that because I had given mission work as the reason for my visit to Ghana the police considered me a spy. I'll admit that I lost my temper and finally, after signing many papers, I ran all the way to the plane, boarding just before they closed the door.

When we were in the air, we were told that we would be making an unscheduled stop in Gambia. The people from Gambia told us that they were being evacuated because the plane that was supposed to pick them up had received a bomb threat. We flew a while longer, and then started a descent over the Atlantic Ocean. The pilot came on the intercom to say that we were making a stop in the Cape Verde Islands. Once we were on the ground, we were told that everyone and everything on the plane was going to be removed and a thorough search of the plane would be made. We went to a small airport where there were armed military and police everywhere. Each person on the plane was photographed and searched. No food or drinks were offered for the several hours that we were there. This was the only trip to Ghana where I spent all my money in Ghana and had nothing but some Canadian money left. The airport would not accept anything but American dollars, so I had nothing to eat or drink. We then had to reclaim our luggage and board the plane again. When we took off, there were three pieces of unclaimed luggage sitting on the tarmac. The sight of those unclaimed bags gave me an unsettled feeling.

However, this is not the end of the story. The plane had not been serviced with food or drinks, so for the trip back to New York there was no food or water, only warm Coke to drink. I never drink Coke, but I had no choice. They did not clean out the toilets at this airport either, so the closer we got to North America the worse the smell became. But in this case, I was glad I didn't have food in my stomach!

When we neared New York, the pilot came on the intercom again to say that there was a bad storm in New York and no planes were being allowed to land and that we were being rerouted to Boston. I thought this is good; I'll be able to get my connecting flight to Ottawa and get home. When we landed in Boston, there was no Customs service for overseas flights so they wouldn't let anyone off the plane. There was a riot among the passengers with people fighting and trying to exit the plane. The police were called and anyone who left the plane was arrested. The plane was moved to the very edge of the airport property and guarded with police. After about three hours they announced that the storm that had closed New York was headed to Boston, so we had to take off to avoid getting caught in the storm. We flew back to New York and were allowed to land. By this time, it was very late, and Air France, the parent company of Air Afrique, only had one counter person to try to reroute a whole planeload of people. Anyone that had made the reservations themselves on the internet had to find their own accommodations. However, I had made mine through a travel agency; so at two a.m., with all my luggage, I was taken into the city and put up in a hotel for four hours.

In the morning, I was taken back to the airport and rerouted to Boston and Ottawa. When I went to board the plane, I discovered that the flight had been cancelled because there were not enough people for the flight. After making my third collect phone call to my husband Lorne, they re booked my flight to Boston and Ottawa. Once again, when I went to the gate to board, I was told the flight had been cancelled. Finally, after losing my temper again, they found me a seat on the last flight to Boston. I called Lorne again and got on the plane.

To add insult to injury, there was a very large man on the flight sitting on the same side as I on the small turboprop plane. The stewardess came to ask me to change to the other side to balance the plane. I was not happy, but I was so tired that I couldn't even speak. Because it was a short flight, there was no food. I had four packages of cookies and three drinks.

By the end of my travels, the actual flight time was forty-eight hours, the longest flight I have ever had anywhere. When we arrived in Ottawa, my luggage wasn't there. And Lorne was not in a good mood after three trips to Ottawa to pick me up, to say nothing of the parking bill of thirty-three dollars. I described my luggage to the attendant and left. Lorne had brought a coat and blanket, so I slept all the way home. Three days later, my luggage arrived at my home in the middle of the night and was left on my steps. I vowed I would never fly Air France again.

Chapter 12

Help is on the Way! The CIDA Youth Internship Program Starting

As part of the funding from the *Canadian International Development Agency* (*CIDA*), *Project Reach Out Canada* was able to access the *CIDA* Youth Internship program through *HelpAge Canada (HAC)*. I was asked to take part in the interview process for the interns being considered for both *Project Reach Out,* and a volunteer with *Help the Aged Ghana*. Roxanne Struk was the first intern to be accepted for the agroforestry project with *PRO*.

In November 2000, I was set to travel to Ghana again, and Roxanne travelled with me. We met at Pearson Airport in Toronto. My luggage was overweight again, and I had to redistribute some things to Roxanne's luggage and throw away two boxes of children's cough syrup—which we really needed for the clinics in Ghana. With many delays in Toronto because of bad weather, we were late taking off. However this meant there was a very short wait time in Amsterdam.

Arriving in Ghana, we discovered that the *PRO* building projects were started, funded by *CIDA* matching grants. The *PRO*

Roxanne Struk and Dan Quarshie

headquarters, a three-room building on the Sakumono church property, was finished. It included an office for Joe Ocran in his capacity of International director of *PRO*, an office for his secretary, Faustina Yalley and a room that served as a library. Construction on the ten-room Ashiyie Community Clinic had also started.

An agroforestry officer, Dan Quarshie had been hired by *PRO Ghana,* and he travelled with us to Ashiyie. From the building site of the Ashiyie Clinic, we continued down the Dodowa Road to the village of Ayikumi. A ten-acre plot of land, rented on a twenty-year lease, was slated be a demonstration farm and tree nursery. Mahogany trees are planted every ten feet around the property to mark its boundaries. When the lease is up, these trees will be harvested and the wood will be sold. The CIDA funding provided for the building of a three-room farmhouse on the property. Acacia and mango trees have been planted, along with a crop of okra and white beans between the trees as a cash crop.

On November sixteenth, we travelled to the villages of Otrokpe and Bomase, where we gave out primary school scholarships to fourteen orphan students who had no one to pay their school fees. The village of Bomase welcomed us with a big parade and a tribal ceremony.

On the seventeenth, the clinic van picked me up, and we travelled to four villages. Sunday, November nineteenth, we headed for the city of Ho near the Eastern border with Togo. Neither Dr. Darko nor Dr. Arthur could go with us on this trip, so we had no doctor for the clinic. When we got to Ho, Joe preached at the church service and then Pastor Luis introduced us to his Ziga group. They were a group of Trokosi children he had rescued from the streets, and he was housing and training them. (Chapter thirteen outlines the history of the Klefe Vocational School.) He organized the girls into a singing group and the boys into a drumming group. They performed for us, and Jemima presented the drumming group with a set of drums and a talking drum.

After the presentation, we held a medical clinic. We found a retired male nurse who translated for us for one hundred and seventeen registered people. It was late when we started, so we

Traditional tribal ceremony at Bomase

didn't have time to see them all. There were many older people here. One patient was a blind boy; we were able to make arrangements for him to be seen by a specialist in the Accra area.

Roxanne spent her days touring different areas of the Greater Accra area, learning about the vegetation, rainfall, and other things that are part of her agroforestry training. At the end of each week, both Roxanne and I sent off our reports to Help Age Canada and CIDA. I continued travelling with the staff on the medical clinic van.

Roxanne wanted to take a hike to the Shai Hills baboon reserve. I reluctantly accompanied her as Jemima would not let her go alone with the Ghanaian male guides. We saw some interesting things on that trip, such as snail carcasses. When I asked, the guide said the snakes like to eat them. I'm deathly afraid of snakes, and they are protected in this baboon reserve. "Don't worry," the guide said, "They are afraid of you too." Small comfort! On to a bat cave! You could hear the bats a long way off. There was only one way in and it was through a very narrow slit in the rock. With my backpack off, I was able to slide through the crack with a push from behind and a pull from the guide ahead of me. We had nothing to eat until we got back through that crack in the rock. History says that in ancient times, people lived up in these Shai hills. It is hard to believe that a community could exist in this primitive area.

Sunday, December third, we headed for Tuakwa/Empiro for church and a clinic. We saw one hundred fifty people, many of whom were young people. Many in this area have Bilharzia, a water-borne parasitic disease that attacks the kidneys. We also saw several with epilepsy, some suspected AIDS cases, and treated a woman with pneumonia. Roxanne provided first aid for many skin sores.

A house was found for Roxanne. She had been staying with Joe and Jemima. She intended to stay in Ghana for about seven months. December seventh is election day in Ghana. Albert Ocran had been studying in Canada and was on his way home to Ghana for the Christmas vacation. His plane was coming into Amsterdam from Canada at the same time as mine was arriving from Ghana, so we were able to meet at the airport and visit until it was time for our planes to load to take us both to our destinations. It would be a rush at home to get ready for Christmas!

The first building housed the sewing, batik and tie-dye classes

The second building for carpentry and trades

Chapter 13

The History of the Klefe Vocational School

In 2000, *Project Reach Out Ghana* travelled to the Ho district in Eastern Ghana to hold a church service and a medical clinic. The pastor at the time, Pastor Luis, had been working with the youth of the town. He was very concerned with the growing number of "Trokosi" children on the streets. These children were given to the fetish priest as payment for the sins of the family and the parents. The priests took the girls as wives and concubines and pressed the boys into servitude. Christian organizations negotiated with the fetish priests, paying them to release some of the children. Once the children were released, they needed to be taught marketable skills.

Pastor Luis collected these girls off the street and housed them in a dormitory-style home he had rented and started an educational program. He started a sewing course for the girls and a farming project to teach the boys some agricultural skills. He also started a kente-weaving course. The courses took place in a rented house and the Klefe Vocational School was born with twenty-four students.

Project Reach Out became responsible for this small school. Several years went by. Eventually, enough money was raised to purchase a ten-acre property in Klefe, a suburb of Ho, and erect the first building. A kente-weaving teacher and a sewing teacher were hired, and courses started in earnest. Later, fabric design, tie-dye, and batik courses were added. Some products from this school were brought to Canada and sold at our Ghana markets; including market bags, back packs, placemats, and napkins—all crafted from batik and tie-dye fabrics made by the students in the sewing classes.

After a couple of years, a construction teacher was hired and a few students came to take this course. We recognized there was not enough space to teach the courses we envisioned for the future. Bringing electricity into the property was very expensive, but it was needed. We started fundraising so we could build a second structure to teach the building trades.

When Lorne Tanney died, In Memoriam donations were directed to this fund. Eventually, after weather related delays, construction resumed, and the second building was completed.

Currently, a partnership has developed between *Project Reach Out Ghana*, the community of Klefe and The Department of Social Welfare and the National Vocational and Technical Institute. Students are tested by the Vocational and Technical Institute. When they complete their three-year courses, they are issued government licenses, allowing them to obtain jobs and provide a source of income for themselves and their families.

The courses currently being offered to up to sixty-five students are: Sewing and Dressmaking, Secretarial and Office Procedures; English and Math; Computers; Electrical One; Electrical Two; Electrical Installation; and Building Construction (masonry and carpentry).

Kenti weaving

Chapter 14

What Good is a One Day Clinic?

People have asked me what does a one-day clinic really do to help sick people since there is no follow-up.

It was a small clinic in the village of Tuakwa; we only saw one hundred fifty people after the morning church service, which was held in a school classroom. At this clinic, we had a doctor and a nurse from Tema with us. With an interpreter, I interviewed people to find out why they had come to see the doctor and to check their vital signs and list their complaints. They then saw the doctor, were given a prescription, and were sent to the medication table where the nurse from Tema dispensed any medications that were prescribed.

When the clinic finished, there were a few still waiting to be seen by the doctor. I saw a woman struggling to walk up a slight incline to reach the registration table. She had to stop to rest and catch her breath every few steps. When she reached the registration table, she was told that the clinic was finished. I watched as she sat down heavily on a rock. Her breathing was laboured as she sat crying. I went over to her, felt her pulse, which was fast, and felt her forehead, which was warm. She was crying and gasping for breath with noisy respirations and begging with her eyes to be seen. I took her by the hand and guided her to the line where the doctor was finishing interviewing patients. "Carole,

I told you that we can't see any more people," he said. "Please, doctor, just this one more lady. If she doesn't have pneumonia I'll eat my shirt," I said. He had never heard that saying before and laughed loudly. "Alright—one more," he agreed.

On the way home, he said, "Your shirt is safe, Carole!" and went on to say the woman had been so congested with pneumonia that she would have died in a few days without the antibiotic he prescribed.

Now scroll ahead five years. We were back in that same village for another clinic after the Sunday morning church service. During the service, I watched three women sitting to the side of the classroom. They were talking during the service and pointing at the visitors. All the visitors were seated at the front of the room. After the service, I asked Jemima if she could find out why they were pointing at me and talking. During the clinic, the woman who had been pointing came through the line and shook my hand and curtsied to me. After the clinic on the way home, Jemima told me that the women were talking about me as the nurse who was at the clinic five years earlier. Apparently, this was the same woman who I had taken to the doctor, who had been diagnosed with pneumonia and given the antibiotic.

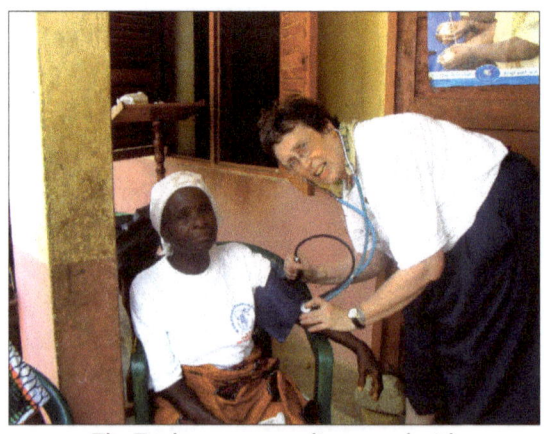

The Tuakwa woman diagnosed with pneumonia five years before

For those who wonder if we actually make a difference in a one-day clinic, I say an empathic YES! To that woman, we made a huge difference. We do make a difference for many children with preventable diseases; and for pregnant women who are given folic acid, iron, and vitamins to improve their own health and the health of their unborn babies.

We do make a difference!

Chapter 15

Very Memorable 2002 Trip

So many mishaps but so many pleasures! Only a missions trip could have so many things go wrong but still be a success.

The 2002 trip started with me traveling alone to Ghana; I arrived on June twenty-third so that I could be there to help Jemima get ready for the arrival of the rest of the team for the opening of the Ashiyie Community Clinic. Joe was still in Canada, and Jemima was very tired. There were many trips to Accra and Ashiyie making arrangements for the clinic opening. Jemima and I decided that I would take her away for a few days of rest before the rest of the team arrived. Joe arrived home from Canada on June twenty-fifth.

On June twenty-eighth, we went to Paradise Ment Hotel near Ada for a short rest. On the way we came on a terrible trotro (local van/bus) accident. We stopped to help, providing first aid to many people. Both Jemima and I had first aid kits in the car. One man's arm was almost completely severed. I had a bottle of purified water that I was going to use to try to clean his wounds, when a woman grabbed the bottle and poured it over her head. Other cars came along to help with the injured and take them to a hospital down the road. Only one day to rest and walk on the beach then back to Tema for Joe to be back for a pastors' meeting.

Diella had a dog named "Shalom," but he didn't like me and he certainly was not very "peaceful." On my way to the outdoor shower, Shalom bit my arm, and I still bear the scar!

I had been to choir practices with Jemima, so the group asked me to sing with them and even had a matching choir dress made for me. I sang phonetically in the Twi language.

We were invited to the Canadian High Commission for Canada Day celebrations. On July fourth, Jemima and I went to Anomabo Beach Resort near Cape Coast for two days of rest.

An apartment rented for the CIDA Youth Interns was empty, so we cleaned it and got it ready for the team to stay there. I went with the mobile clinic van during the day to assist at clinics. On Monday, we went to the Tema Oil refinery for a clinic for the truck drivers, and on Wednesday to the Togo Road oil refinery.

On July tenth, Sherrie (Rounding) Davis and Darren Croswell arrived from Canada. Sheldon and Stephanie Gilmer arrived on the eleventh and Mbio Kutake from DR Congo on the thirteenth. The Gilmers stayed with Joe and Jemima and the rest of us stayed at the apartment. When we arrived at the apartment, there was an angry crowd chasing a man with a machete. We decided to go to Joe and Jemima's house until things cooled down.

Sunday, July fourteenth, after church in the morning, Joe, Mbio, Stephanie and Sheldon drove in one vehicle; and Sherrie, Darren, clinic nurse Maggie, and I went in the clinic van driven by Kudjo, headed for Northern Ghana. We drove to Kumasi but were late getting there. The reserved rooms at the guest house had been given to someone else, and we had to sleep on pieces of foam on the floor. To top it all off, the water was off. Stephanie and Sheldon were the only ones to get a bed. We decided to try and go to Mole National Park to the elephant reserve on our way. The road was unbelievably bad; however, we did see the elephants and started back to go to Tamale. There had been some trouble between chiefs in the area and there was a curfew of nine p.m., after which the barriers to the city would be closed, and no one could get in.

Elephant at Mole National Park

In our rush to get to the barriers before nine p.m., we had a flat tire. Even though the men changed it in record time, we were twenty minutes late to the barrier, and no amount of talking would convince the guards to raise the barrier and let us through.

So what to do? We had a snack and sang *How Great Thou Art*, prayed, and tried to go to sleep. Sherrie and Stephanie lay across the seats of the Toyota. Sheldon and Mbio bedded down in the ditch beside the vehicles, while Joc and Darren tried to sleep in the reclining front seats of the mobile clinic with Maggie across the second seat, and me across the back seat. Kudjo guarded us all, sitting on the back bumper of the van. A van load of Muslims arrived at the barrier just after us, and they were not happy that we sang and prayed. They all laid down on the road behind our vehicles.

At five a.m. they opened up the barriers, and we went on to Tamale. Joe had often stayed at the Akam Guest House, so we went there to shower, and change clothes. Then we left for Salaga. What a terrible road! Joe took the tire to be fixed, and the rest of us walked around Salaga. Sherrie was taking a picture and stepped back, not knowing that there was a drop-off. She fell off the road, hitting her head on the pavement. She was knocked out and had a serious cut to her scalp plus injuries to her arms and leg. We found some ice and left the area quickly as a crowd was gathering. The guest house that Joe had reserved turned out to be unsuitable, but we were fortunate to find another guest house with room for all of us. After spraying all the rooms with Raid and Lysol, we settled in for the night.

Next day, we went to Sabonjida, one hour's drive away (but only twenty-four kilometres), where Pastor Stephen had organized a clinic. Two hundred eighty people registered. A local nurse who was helping us decided to take a two-hour lunch break but we kept going. Stephanie and Sherrie packaged medications, Maggie dispensed the drugs, and I assessed people. Sheldon and Mbio interviewed the chiefs, and Darren interviewed pastors. We also gave out school supplies. After spending another night in our guest house, we left for home. We were supposed to take the ferry on our return trip, cutting off several hours of travel time; but because of low water levels, the ferry couldn't dock—so we had to take the terrible road back to Tamale to stay at the Akam Guest House. The van was not working well due to dirty fuel and fuel pump problems. We drove fourteen hours all the way back to Tema. Too tired to unpack, we just showered and fell into bed.

Opening day at Ashiyie Community Clinic

There was much to do before the opening of the clinic on July nineteenth. Jemima had worked very hard while we were in the north, and the clinic looked beautiful. The Police Band provided the music. Two TV stations were there to report the event. Louise, from the Canadian High Commission, did the ribbon cutting, and many important people attended—including the Minister of Health, the Police Commissioner, and chiefs. Lots of pictures were taken. All in all it was a very tiring but successful day!

Saturday, July twentieth was Joe's birthday, and Jemima had a birthday party for him. July twenty-third, Stephanie and Sheldon left to fly home. Mbio left on the twenty-fourth. We all put things together for him to take back to Congo to his family. Sherrie and Darren left on the twenty-fifth.

Sheldon, Joe, and I tested positive for malaria and had to take the treatment. When I went to Ashiyie Clinic to be tested, Jackson, the lab technician, educated me about malaria. He got out the lab book and made me read about diagnosing malaria and, when he put the slide under the microscope, he asked what I saw. The answer? I had stage two malaria. He gave me the necessary treatment. The last day of medication was the day I was to leave Ghana.

I was supposed to leave on the twenty-eighth, but the flight was cancelled; I was eventually able to get a seat on the twenty-ninth. I was so weak from malaria that I couldn't get up the stairs into the plane; the staff had to help me up. In Amsterdam, I was on standby status for the flight to Toronto because of the flight cancellation on the twenty-eighth. At the last minute, I was able to get a seat. Because a passenger was late and they had already started to unload his luggage, we lost our place in the air-traffic take-off pattern. We were so late taking off that England wouldn't let us fly in their air space, so we had to have a new flight plan to fly over Norway—taking an hour longer.

We finally landed safely in Toronto. I slept the whole way on the airport bus from Toronto to Kingston, arriving at eleven p.m. Lorne was there to pick me up, and I slept the rest of the way to Brockville. It took a whole week for me to get rested and adjust to the time difference. I had a repeat test at home for malaria and it was negative. Praise God, the treatment did its job. Through celebrations, travels, and illness, God took care of us again.

Chapter 16

A Life-Long Dream— September/October 2003

A trip to Africa is a lifelong dream for some people. It was that way for Janet Roth, a nurse from Oshawa. She had often talked about her wish to go to Africa so her pastor, Brian Bertrim called me to see if there was a possibility of her going with me. Things all worked out for her to travel with me that year. Nature did have a say in the plans as her plane couldn't take off from Toronto, and we weren't able to meet in London. I went on to Ghana alone, and she arrived the next day.

Three CIDA youth interns were in Ghana that year: Anne Babcock in gerontology, Danielle Lefevbre in agroforestry with PRO and Ami Somani with *Help Age Ghana* in gerontology.

Laura Swift from Brockville had gone to Ghana on a university exchange program. The first night she was there, she was robbed of everything of value; passport, health card, money, etc. Her mother was a teacher in Brockville and found out through Faye Croswell that I was going to Ghana. She asked me if I would take the replacement items to Laura. I met with Laura twice while I was in Ghana. Such a nice young woman and she certainly was appreciative of the money and passport that I brought from home.

Some interesting things that took place on this trip:

- We couldn't get rid of the ants in our bed—ones that bite and sting; also red ants in our luggage, purses, and clothes. We bought ant and roach spray.
- Two CIDA interns, plus Janet and myself, took a malaria training program sponsored by the British Women's group.
- I got a marriage proposal from an old guy at the malaria training sessions!

PRO village cooperatives for the elderly have started, and we visited several. The cooperatives must have at least ten people over the age of fifty and each has access to a minimum of a half acre of land. *PRO* gives each person enough acacia trees to plant, three meters apart, as an agroforestry project. It takes three years for the trees to mature enough to be cut down for firewood; either for sale, or for family use. When the trees regrow from the stumps, another crop of wood can be harvested in another three years. Residents were also each given a couple of mango tree seedlings to help the family with food and income.

Janet and I both worked at Ashiyie Clinic several times doing maternal and child-care clinics, and advocacy for the elderly clinics. We also provided first aid at Anum School.

We headed for Northern Ghana, where we visited Kintampo Falls and walked down one hundred fifty steps to see the Falls—and then had to climb back up!

We started down the road to Mole National Park. The road was terrible with many potholes. About half-way to the park, Joe hit a huge pothole, and both tires on the left side of the vehicle went flat with rims bent. We only had one spare tire, so we walked about a kilometre to the nearby village of Mempeasem, which means, "I don't want trouble." There were no vehicles or tires in the village. We sat on

The Village of Mempeamese

a log and sang songs with the children; everyone in the village came to see us. They offered us the cement floor of the school to sleep on; but we decided to stay in our car, a five-seat Toyota packed to the roof, with a space made for the sixth person to sit in the back. Six people create a lot of moisture! When we put the windows up, they got steamed—and when we put them down the mosquitoes came in by droves! The Muslim minaret beside the car started call to prayer at four-thirty a.m. A man on a motor bike took our tire to Domango and Joe and Jemima took a very early local bus.

Someone found a tire on a Toyota somewhere and brought it to us, but Joe and Jemima weren't back, so I drove all of us in the vehicle towards Domango—stopping every vehicle along the way to try to find Joe and Jemima. They finally came along in a taxi and we went on to Domango to buy a tire and give back the borrowed one. By this point, it was too late to go on to Mole park. No elephants this trip. We drove back the way we came and on to Tamale to Akam guest house. I have never been so dirty. My hair was red from the road dust. Three of us ended up with malaria from this experience.

After a full night's sleep, we drove to Salaga and Sabonjida and then back to Tamale over that terrible road again.

More interesting things on this trip:

- We travelled to Bukyondo to do a clinic. We were supposed to be there the day before. Over five hundred people had waited all day. The day we arrived, only about two hundred showed up. With all of us working, we saw everyone. It was the rainy, flooding season, so getting to the village meant we had to drive through water. On the return trip, the vehicle stopped and we couldn't get it to go. We suspected there could be water in the oil, as there was lots of white smoke. The two pastors went for help. The rest of us sat in the vehicle and ate the supper Frances had prepared for us. After getting back on the road to Accra, we had another flat tire.

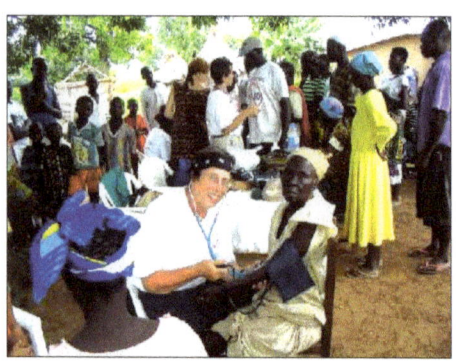

The clinic under the mamgo tree

- We attended a wedding that lasted three-and-a-half hours.

- We met with Dr. Nana Apt, a world famous gerontologist, about issues for the elderly in Ghana, and to plan her appearance on *PRO's* radio broadcast.

- I developed a bad cold with lots of coughing. On the return trip to Canada, they sprayed the plane twice—perhaps in an attempt to kill all the bacteria from my coughing.

- I had a twelve-hour wait at Heathrow for my flight to

Montreal. Janet only had a seven-hour wait for her plane to Toronto.

- We are thankful to God for another safe and event-filled trip to Ghana.

Reflections from Ami Somani, CIDA Youth Intern

Flooded road that we had to drive through

"My time in Ghana was significant in the traditional sense of making lifelong friends, absorbing a new culture, and learning to work with challenging resources; but it also taught me about myself and my strengths. It taught me about the power of laughter and human connection, and it lit in my heart a fire of compassion that drives me—to this day—to help others through health and education."

Reflection from Janet Roth

"It had always been a dream of mine to go to Africa. When I shared this with my pastor, he said he would look into it. Six months later, I was on a plane to Ghana, West Africa.

"I don't think I will ever forget the first church experience I had in Ghana. I did not understand what was being said as the sermon was in Twi. However, I didn't really need to. I was in awe as I looked around at the faces of the people, all in their Sunday best, as they listened, as they sang, and as they danced.

"Preparations for our mobile clinic in remote areas of the northern region of Ghana were an adventure in themselves; but they were times I will always remember and cherish. We spent time packaging medications and packing our vehicle in preparation for our long drive—six of us and all our supplies. The roads initially were good. As we drove longer, and into more remote areas, the roads became much worse. Travelling along the very bumpy roads and avoiding goats in the dark, we suddenly came down with a bang and found ourselves with not one, but two flat tires, on an isolated dirt road. In Ghana, you cannot call CAA to come and help you. In fact, there were no cell phone signals where we were. We got out and a young man on a bicycle came and helped us out. We followed him to a village almost a mile away. After a sleepless night in the car, and as the day progressed and we had time for prayer, we thought of our families at home on that Thanksgiving Day. I remember being a bit weepy, and Jemima came to me and told me that God had a purpose for me and there was a reason for me being there. We did make it to our clinic and saw over 100 people.

"There was so much I learned and enjoyed from this experience: to not only tolerate but enjoy cold water showers; to be patient when I turned on a light switch to wait to see if the lights would come on; how to adapt to no electricity and how to conserve the precious water; breakdowns are not necessarily a bad thing. In fact, I came to enjoy them as each came with an incredibly unique experience where we got to spend time with the wonderful people in the area. I made amazing lifelong friends with Carole, Ami and Anne, and of course with Joe Ocran and his beautiful wife whom I lovingly call my twin sister, Jemima.

"Ghana will always hold a special place in my heart. My experiences have been nothing but positive and ones I will always cherish. I find that each time I go, it is like recharging my batteries, I am renewed spiritually and emotionally. I have learned not to take things for granted and learned to be thankful for all that we have in life. I remember after service one day, a young man coming to me saying he just didn't understand why we would come all the way from Canada to help people in Ghana, people we didn't know. He said 'what an amazing God we have'. Yes indeed, what an amazing God we have."

Chapter 17
2004 –
Death Seems to be Following Us

On October twenty-fourth, four women left Canada for Ghana: Janet Roth from Toronto, Tali Alexander, Marjorie McCullough and me from Ottawa/Montreal. Tali was traveling with us for a six-month stay at a village near Asamankese to work in the Osanese orphanage. Before we arrived in Ghana, the Badu family who ran the orphanage were in a car accident on the way home from a family funeral, and the wife and daughter were killed in the accident. The husband was seriously injured and in hospital. As a result, Tali could not go ahead to the orphanage, so she stayed with us in Tema. Her friend Charles tried to make arrangements for her to stay with some of his family but that didn't work out.

Carole, Tali, Marjorie, and Janet

There were three CIDA youth interns with *Project Reach Out* this year staying in the apartment, so our group was divided with Marjorie and Janet staying with Joe and Jemima, and Tali and me staying at the apartment with the interns; Sharada Keates,

Jillian Watkins, and Amanda Quinn. On behalf of *Project Reach Out*, we visited *Help Age Ghana* and several government people and made arrangements for our radio broadcasts about issues involving the elderly. This broadcast on ADOM radio dealt with advocacy for the elderly, human rights issues, disease processes, and women's rights in old age. The broadcast had the potential to reach three million people in three language groups and was made possible by the CIDA matching funds grant.

We learned some health facts from these interviews. Tema has the largest incidence of HIV/AIDS in Ghana. This is because of people from many countries enter Ghana through the port. The truckers come to the port from Burkina Faso, Mali, and Ivory Coast. However, the incidence is much lower than any other country in West Africa. There was a large polio immunization project this month in Ghana.

Jemima got a call on the evening of October twenty-eighth that her mother had died. She and her "sisters" (really her cousins), left to go to the rest of the family in Kofoidua.

The team and the interns spent time at the Ashiyie clinic assisting in the Well Baby clinics, attending the gerontology education classes being held in different villages, and visiting agroforestry cooperative participants. We also traveled to visit Anum school with its two hundred fifteen students, and Klefe Vocational School, where the building is almost complete. Classes are in progress even though the school is not complete.

The CIDA matching grants provided funding to send containers of supplies to Ghana. Many institutions and people provided medical supplies, bikes, tractors, a motorcycle, school supplies, and items for Joe and Jemima to use in the ministry.

In the summer of 2004, *PRO Canada* shipped a container of medical, agroforestry and educational supplies, including twenty computers donated by Thousand Islands Secondary School in Brockville. The container arrived in Tema port on Saturday, the thirtieth. We went to help unload the container and load it into a storage container. One of the men helping to unload the container tried to steal a bicycle and some other things. A bystander saw him, told Jemima, and she ran after him—actually catching him and bringing back the items.

The gerontology education class in Frafraha

The 2004 team packing the container in Canada

Pictures show Marjorie, Janet and Carole helping to unload the container.

Sunday, October thirty-first, we attended the funeral of the chief of

2005 team packing containers

103

Driving the donated tractor into the container

Carole helping to unload the container

Marjorie helping

Janet

Ashalley-Botwe. He had been the one to arrange for the property for the Ashalley-Botwe church and the *PRO* daycare school. We had to have special funeral clothes made.

Wednesday, November third, we drove to Korfoidua for the wake for Jemima's mother. While we were gone, Tali moved out and drove to Osenase to start her work at the orphanage.

Ian Wagg, the son of a Brockville doctor, was doing an exchange program at the University of Ghana, and we were able to get together several times. Ian was planning on becoming a doctor too. He even came to the airport when we left to see us off.

Monday, November eighth, we drove all the way to Mole National Park in Northern Ghana and had many serious accidents along the way. We took two vehicles: Joe,

Marjorie, Janet, and me went in one car; and Pastor Isaac, Dorothy, clinic nurse, and driver, Eric, went in the *PRO* Toyota truck. We stayed overnight at the park and saw the elephants the next morning. When we stopped at the junction on

Ian and Carole at the airport

the way to Tamale, a woman approached us and gave Marjorie a baby that was about a month old. She was insistent that we take the baby back to America. After making sure the woman understood that we could not take the baby, we drove through Tamale and then on to Salaga with a side trip to Buymondo school. This school was later taken over by the government. The next day we drove to Sabonjida and then on to Kabeso where *PRO* was building a clinic. It was not quite finished, but we held a clinic there anyway. The team treated about one hundred twenty-six people. Marjorie took temperatures and held babies, while Janet and I did assessments and nurse Dorothy manned the medication table.

At one of the villages, someone gave Joe a goat as a gift. He tied it to the supports in the back of the Toyota truck, and we all took off to drive back to Tamale. The car was following the truck, but

Marjorie and Carole

105

due to the terribly rutted road, the car fell behind. As we were driving past a village, there was a goat standing in the middle of the road. I said, "That looks like the goat Joe was given as a gift." When we got to Tamale, Joe went to untie the goat—and it was gone. The answer was probably that the road was so rough that the goat became untied and was knocked out of the truck bed, but we teased Joe mercilessly that he tossed a goat. It became a fun story to tell subsequent teams.

Thursday, the eleventh, we drove the fourteen-hour trip back to Tema, with several pit stops and car-sickness stops.

When it came time to head for home on Friday, November twelfth, it was fifty degrees Celsius in the sun and thirty-one in the house. Janet decided that she would stay with Jemima until her mother's funeral was over. Neither Marjorie or I were able to do that, so we headed for the airport. They said I couldn't take my carry-on bag on the plane because it was too heavy; so after we got through inspection, I transferred some things to Marjorie's bag and took off the tags Customs had attached. I then carried the bag onto the plane with no problem.

We shopped for Christmas gifts in the Amsterdam airport. Marjorie's husband, Conrad, and their children were at the airport in Montreal to meet us. We went out for supper and then drove home to Brockville. Marjorie brought her family up-to-date on all the events of our trip and I slept most of the way.

Chapter 18

We Need a Dentist– 2005 Team

At many clinics in the last ten years, we have seen the need for dental care—especially among the older population. At Centennial Road Standard Church, we had several dentists. As I talked about the need, two of them came forward to discuss the possibility of making a missions trip to Ghana. A lot of planning was needed— in fact, about a year of planning.

The 2005 dental team

Dr. Barbara Wahn and Dr. Mark Stevens started talking about what they would need. They convinced one of Barb's classmates, Dr. Lawrence Reimer, from Swift Current, Saskatchewan, to join us. Three dental assistants—Lisa MacCaffrey, Karen Sharpe, and Monika Heron were added to the team, as was dental hygienist Linda Owen. Barb's sister, Linda Maloney, a nurse, and Barb's husband, Ian, an accountant who did all the sterilization for the dental clinics joined the team, as did Ed Hyatt, a pastor friend of Lawrence Reimer's. There were eleven of us in total. This was the largest team I have ever taken to Ghana and the first team where all the costs of the trip were paid in advance of leaving Canada.

Drs. Lawrence, Barb and Mark with dentist from Saskatchewan

The dentists made lists of things they would need, and when everything was collected, a large crate was shipped to Ghana three months before we left. The dentists paid for all the supplies they would be using. Three portable dental chairs were purchased and put into suitcases. Finally, on April eighth, a van piled high with luggage, and nine of us left for Montreal. Lawrence and Ed flew from Saskatoon. We all met in Amsterdam where nine of us went on a canal boat cruise.

When people travel on these missions teams, everyone pays their own expenses or, if they have financial constraints, they do some fundraising within their own family and social circles. Because of some health problems, the dentists requested that we stay only in five-star hotels. The extra cost was a problem for me as I couldn't afford it. However, the dentists generously covered the extra cost of my hotels. We stayed two in a room at the Mensvic Hotel in Accra, a beautiful, modern hotel. There were many of us in addition to our Ghanaian travel partners and the luggage needed for the clinics, so we had to rent a large bus.

Sunday, April tenth was our first full day in Ghana. We went to Sakumono Church for morning service. It was a pleasant surprise to have a dentist and his wife from Saskatchewan come to the church to greet and visit with us. That day was Jemima's birthday, so we all met in the hotel dining room later for dinner and a birthday party.

The first day of the clinic went fairly slowly with unpacking supplies and set up. Unfortunately, the preparation that was supposed to have been done ahead of time had not happened. We were buying bottled water by the case and I suggested that each person drink at least one-and-a-half, two-litre bottles of water a day. Everyone drank more than they expected they could. It was very hot. Betty Lemstra had been in Ghana assisting Joe Ocran in the ministry of the church. She took Linda Owen to the schools to set up appointments for her to return and teach students proper dental hygiene and flossing techniques. Over the next several days, she taught over four hundred students and gave out toothbrushes and dental floss.

Some highlights of our days:

- Doing only extractions: Mark did a very complex surgical extraction painlessly; Barb performed a really difficult extraction; one patient had four teeth extracted; one ninety year old lady who had never seen a dentist and had been in pain a long time, kissed Barb's hand and thanked her.
- Over 300 extractions and only one person fainted!
- Karen was left behind when the bus left because she had been playing with some kids. When we missed her, we went back and found her

- The bus driver was stopped for speeding. They tried to take him to jail until he paid the fine. We paid it from team money.

- When the girls went shopping, Karen fell through a broken sewer grate in the sidewalk. We did some first-aid and went on shopping.

- We held five days of clinics at the Ashiyie Community clinic, two at Ashalley-Botwe Kindercare School and then a clinic in the village of Tuakwa after church on Sunday. At one Ashalley-Botwe clinic the thermometer read over fifty degrees Celsius in the sun and thirty-one in the room where the dentists were working. We were very thankful for borrowed electric fans!

- One woman was so happy to have her tooth pulled that she did a dance outside the room where the Tuakwa clinic was held.

- Ian Wagg, an exchange university student from Brockville, came with us one to an Ashiyie Clinic one day and had supper with us another day. He was studying at the University of Ghana.

- Every evening we got together for devotions. One evening we held a very special communion service with special prayer for all our families at home.

- We visited St. George's Castle at Elmina, a slave castle built by the Portuguese in 1482.

- We took shopping trips for souvenirs for ourselves, our families, and for the Ghana Market. (We sell Ghanaian items in Canada at the Ghana Market there, and send the money back to Ghana to help fund the projects.)

After fourteen days in Ghana, all the team left for home except me. I went to Joe and Jemima's home. It was very hot with only a ceiling fan and no air conditioning, over thirty eight Celsius in the room and forty two Celsius outside. I was very thankful that the electricity didn't go off.

When all the accounting was done, there was three dollars and forty five cents Canadian left over! With eleven people each paying approximately $3,000 for plane tickets, hotels, food and water, rental of a bus and driver, paying all the expenses for the Ghanaians that accompanied us, all the tips and other incidentals, it was amazing that God supplied all our needs. With prices changing almost daily in Ghana it is almost impossible to predict all the expenses. It truly was a miracle.

Reflections of a dentist: Dr. Barbara Wahn

"The dental mission trip to Ghana in 2005 allowed me to fulfill a calling on my life. Forty years prior to the trip, as a fifteen-year-old, I had felt a call to be a missionary in Africa. Little did I know that I would marry, have two children and become a dentist before it would be fulfilled...but God did! After discussing the dental needs of the people in Ghana with Joe Ocran, I knew it was time. But I needed the expertise of Dr. Lawrence Reimer, a classmate of mine who had been on ten previous dental mission trips, to effectively set up a mobile clinic in a classroom, or open-sided building or under a tree. Yes, we had goats in the doorway, chickens around our feet, and crowds of people watching, chattering and singing as they looked through doorways and glassless windows. We provided portable dental chairs, sufficient anaesthetic, analgesics and antibiotics, gloves, masks and instruments and sterilizing product—two hundred fifty pounds in all. God truly blessed us in these times as we had singing, devotions and prayer morning and evening. Each patient was cared for with an unexpected outpouring of love God gave us for these beautiful strangers who were so grateful for the treatment they received. They were occasionally apprehensive but it was quite touching when they would clutch my hand and say, "God bless you" after I extracted one of their teeth. One woman joyfully danced and waved her arms in the air celebrating her tooth extraction. One fearful seven-year-old boy hastily left the chair, only to return confidently for his treatment after he saw a smile on his four-year-old sister's face following her extraction. God provided the strength to work in extreme heat and humidity with flies everywhere, using hand instruments and head lamps. Success was not measured by the number of teeth extracted, but by the love shown performing the surgery."

"For I hold you by your right hand. I, the Lord your God. And I say to you, 'Don't be afraid. I am here to help you.'" *Isaiah*   *41:13*

"If I gave everything I have to the poor and even sacrificed my body, I could boast about it; but if I didn't have love for others, I would have gained nothing." *I Corinthians 13:13*

Chapter 19
Help!!
There's an Elephant at My Door!
Kanata team 2005

After fourteen days in Ghana, all the first dental team left for home except me. The following day Saturday, April twenty-third, a team from Kanata Wesleyan arrived. They stayed in the apartment that the CIDA youth interns use when they are in Ghana. I remained at

Kanata team: Ann Lillico, Sylvia Summers and Dr. Mark Van Campen

Jemima's. We all went to church together at Asite and heard a very encouraging message from Nehemiah on not becoming discouraged. The Kanata team consisted of Sylvia Summers, a businesswoman, Mark Van Campen, a veterinarian, and Ann Lillico, a nurse. This was a vision-casting team. I took them to the Ashiyie community clinic and to the Ayikume demonstration farm.

Joining the team for the trip to the north on April twenty-sixth was Betty Lemstra (who was in Ghana as a short-term missionary helping in the work of the church), Betty's friend,

Rachel, Pastor Stephen Mensah, and I. We traveled by state bus for fourteen hours to Tamale, Northern Ghana. The *Project Reach Out* ministry van was too small to take all of us with our luggage, so they drove the same route taking our luggage and supplies. When we arrived in Tamale we stayed at the Redach Hotel, built by a friend of Joe's. He was running it as a ministry to reach Muslims by offering free English lessons. The hotel's income, from people like us, funds the ministry.

On Wednesday, April twenty-seventh, we left Tamale by van for Damango and Mole National Park. Ann, Sylvia, and I rented a room in the motel while Betty and Rachel stayed in the hostel. At five-thirty the following morning, we were awakened by Betty, who claimed an elephant was outside her room eating the flowers! We watched as it sauntered around the compound. There were other elephants very close to our motel eating the leaves from the trees. In a National Park, the wild life have free range. There were lots of baboons, monkeys, and warthogs around the property. It was the end of the dry season, so they came out of the bush to find food and water. It was dangerous to get too close to them, so we waited until they went off in another direction.

Elephant at Mole National Park

Then a guide took us in our van for a tour of the park. Unfortunately, it stalled and they couldn't get it going. Our guide hiked back to the park office and brought a car to boost our battery with welcome success. For two-and-a-half hours we drove around the park seeing different kinds of antelope, wild boars, guinea fowl, birds, and of course lots of wild elephants.

After we left the park, about halfway to Damango, the muffler on the van came loose. All we had to re-attach it was a skipping rope, but we managed to tie up the muffler and make it to Damango to have it welded. I have seen some terrible outhouses in my day—but the most disgusting were the public toilets in Damango. Oh my! After some Gravol and Imodium, we were on our way back to Tamale to pick up our suitcases and drive to Salaga. A couple of solar panels had been sent from Canada in a shipment and they were forgotten in Tema, so Joe put them on the bus to Tamale—but someone must have found out what they were, because they never made it. When we arrived in Salaga at the guest house, we got ready for bed and the power went off. Very uncomfortable. Thank goodness I had remembered batteries for my battery-powered fan. It was a God-send!

There was a bad storm in the night, but it cooled the air and the power came back on at six a.m. It is my understanding that they turn off the power when there is a storm coming to prevent damage to the power system.

On Friday we drove to Bukyondu. There were many needs there. They were trying to start a school and build a clinic. They needed cement to cover the mud bricks so they wouldn't be washed away in the rains. The pastor needed a bicycle, many needed clothing, and they definitely needed a building to use as a church. A shipment had been sent from Canada earlier. It included donated soccer uniforms.

When we visited the chief, we found that his son was very sick, so we took them back to Salaga with us to the hospital.

The boys' soccer team decked out in the donated uniforms

We headed for Oando in the afternoon. About one hundred twenty-five people were gathered there under a tree. They asked our team to preach, so Sylvia and Mark both spoke and more than half of the people were led in the sinner's prayer by Pastor Peter Jado, the district leader for the churches in the Salaga district.

We also visited the villages of Boakutido, Gurishe Zongo and Kapioto. There is much potential in these villages. The language in this area is Konkemba, and they need Bibles in their own language.

The following morning we had no water. Someone brought a pail of water so we could flush the toilet. We were buying large bottles of drinking water by the case, so we made do.

Saturday we went to Sabonjida and met with Pastor Stephen and the leaders there. The church that was being built needed a roof; the pastor needed a motorbike, and the district leaders needed bicycles. A member of the church had died and the funeral was in progress, so we paid a visit to the family.

We went on to the village of Kabeso where a clinic was almost ready to be opened. The nurse had been hired, but she was in Accra taking a refresher course. The leaders from the new Tokoro church came to Kabeso. We had a joint meeting with Mark speaking. After the service, we went to an open building next to the church and saw a few sick people. It wasn't a planned clinic, but we did some first-aid. Since he was a vet, Mark was able to diagnose some ailments. We had a few medicines with us that we had brought to donate to the clinic. We saw about forty-five people in that clinic.

Sunday, May first, we started out but needed petrol, and there was none. We found a station that had some in a drum, so we siphoned off eleven gallons—a gallon at a time—pouring it through a rag to filter out the dirt. We then drove to Kakpeni for a service where Sylvia spoke. They gave her a guinea fowl as a gift for speaking. Many blind people, and many needs ,were there. The people requested a church building, Bibles, benches, and lanterns (since they had no electricity). Mark went on a motorbike to visit Kachinke church, and the rest of us went to Buogban for a short service, then on to Beposo. This village was interesting. A young man named Timothy went away to Bible College and came back to his village. All but six people in the village became Christians. They have a bamboo and thatch structure as a church.

We returned to Salaga to pick up our things and eat at Pastor Francis' house and then drove back to Tamale. The muffler fell off again, but we drove on to Tamale. The following morning, Monday, we left the hotel at five a.m. to catch the State bus for the fourteen-hour trip back to Accra. We were all very tired.

We spent a day shopping for souvenirs and things for the Ghana Market. The Kanata team packed up, and after a harried ride in heavy traffic, they made it to the airport and left Ghana. However, my time in Ghana was not quite over.

Joe had a death in his family, so he went to his home village for the wake. I spent the day catching up on laundry, and reconciling receipts for all my spending.

On Saturday, May seventh Jemima was off to another funeral and Joe and I headed out to Klefe to visit the vocational school. It rained every day for a few days so the rainy season had apparently arrived. Dr. and Mrs. Wilson from the Wesleyan church headquarters in Indianapolis, and Lindsay Cameron, Africa Director of Global Partners based in South Africa, all arrived in Ghana en route to Liberia for a conference. We picked them all up at the airport and took them to hotels. On Sunday, Joe went to the hotels and took them to the airport again for the rest of their trip.

Sunday, May eighth was Mother's Day. Sakumono Church had a special service. We took Jemima out for dinner late in the evening. Monday, we visited the *Project Reach Out* projects and visited with Margaret and Joseph Caesar, *PRO* board members.

Delivery of the new-used car motor

We had an unusual experience on Wednesday. We visited a used car parts lot to try to find a motor for Jemima's car. All the car parts were outside in piles. (How they ever find anything, I'll never know.) Jemima bought a motor and used shocks for her Fiat, and took them home and put them in the driveway. Oil leaked all over it, making another big job for her to clean up. Three auto mechanics showed up to get the motor and shocks and had to be transported to a garage to install them. Electricians were at the house putting in new wiring. The power was off, so I couldn't do anything except read and fan myself. Jemima went to collect a parcel from the post office that was mailed December twenty-ninth and received May thirteenth! She had to fill out many forms and pay to get the parcel.

Saturday, May fourteenth there were quick trips to Gbetsile to look at a plot of land for a new *PRO* clinic, and to Dr. Arthur's private clinic called GODIA, meaning "God is Alive." Dr. Arthur is a board member of *PRO Ghana* and has gone on many day clinics with our mobile van over the years. When I was packing to leave, there were small red ants in everything—my clothes, my purse, my suitcase—so I sprayed everything.

Sunday morning, May fifteenth we were off to church. There was a women's meeting after church, so we were late getting home. When I went to my room in the guest house, I discovered that someone had been there and gone through everything—even unpacked my suitcase. All the jewelry I had bought to take back for the Ghana Market, my good dress, my purse with money, my own personal jewelry, my backpack, my thirty-five mm camera, my contact addresses, my gifts for the staff, my battery-operated fan, the school supplies for Anum School, my Via Rail return ticket (I think they thought it was an airline ticket)—even my extra pair of glasses—were all gone. Fortunately, when I was getting ready for church, I had taken my credit card, my driver's license, my digital camera, my airline ticket, and my passport out of my purse, and put them in my fanny pack—so at least I still had what I needed to get on the plane and go home. They even unpacked barrels of Jemima's things that were stored in the room where I was staying. It was a mystery how someone had gotten into the compound over walls topped by broken glass shards, and into my locked room, despite a guard dog on the premises. However, I had no time to investigate as I had to repack and leave for the airport for my trip home. Jemima planned to question the neighbours, and I had a couple of theories. I suspected it could have been the electricians or the neighbours whose house backs onto the back of the guest house at Joe and Jemima's. The wall is a shared wall and could have been broached.

I cleared customs with no difficulty, but there were several extra security checks, even at the top of the ramp before entering the plane. Something was different. The KLM staff said it was a terrorist alert. It was an uneventful flight, but when I got to Montreal, I discovered I had no train ticket back home to Brockville. Thank goodness I had my credit card. I had no money to buy food and the train concessions didn't accept credit cards. I made a claim for the stolen return ticket as my house insurance covered my personal losses. Even with all the events, it was a good productive trip with many reasons to thank God for His provision and protection.

Chapter 20

The Kingston Team—2006

On Friday, March twenty-fourth, 2006, I met five people from Kingston at the Kingston bus terminal to take the airport bus: Lynn and Aiden Rigby, Ruth Brideau, Connie Fellows, and Sue Corcoran. During the KLM fight, there was a medical emergency and we were diverted to Iceland to take a man, who was sitting near me, off the plane. With my nurse's eye, it looked like he was having a breathing problem—maybe an embolism? Many people on the flight missed their connections in Amsterdam, but we still had time to look around before our flight.

Aiden Rigby, Ruth Brideau, Connie Fellows, Sue Corcoran and Carole with Ghanaian helpers

The flight to Accra was interesting, as there was going to be a total eclipse of the sun on March twenty-eighth. The best place in the world to see it would be in Ghana, so many people were flying there for that very purpose. An uneventful trip through

Customs and Immigration was nice. Joe and Jemima were there to meet us with the bus. When they asked at Customs what we were bringing and who we were visiting, I said we were there to visit Rev. Joe Ocran. They said, "Oh Pastor Joe. Go right ahead," and didn't even look into our bags.

We got settled into our guesthouse, the Maruku Hotel. We made our regular visits to a church for Sunday morning service. Then on Monday, we visited the Ashiyie Community Clinic, the Ashalley-Botwe Kindercare School, and the agroforestry farm/tree nursery—with a visit to the Tema market on Tuesday. Wednesday was to be the solar eclipse, and we just had to see that! Many people came to our street. When the sun went totally black, everyone clapped and yelled. After the event, we left for a trip to Anum.

After visiting Anum school, and because it was late in the day, we had to stay in a hotel along the way. There was a difference of opinion on where we should stay. The outcome was that two stayed in a very posh, American-style, expensive hotel on the Volta River, and the rest of us— including the Ghanaians that accompanied us—stayed in a modestly-priced hotel. During the night there was a

Aiden working at Anum School

heavy rain. The power went off and the roof leaked. Something else to add to our experience file! One of the team members was having some issues from an old whiplash injury, so we went with her to the Akosomo Hospital. They wouldn't give her the medication that she requested, and she had not brought it with her from Canada, but we bought a neck brace. She suffered with a lot of pain over the bumpy roads. We went on to visit Klefe Vocational School. On the way back we purchased cement, paint brushes and paint and then went back to Anum School. Aiden worked hard, helping to dig the pilings for the new addition to the school for the Junior Secondary School classrooms. The girls all helped paint the Jane Poelmann Memorial classroom. Carole provided first aid for the students and staff, and restocked their first aid kit.

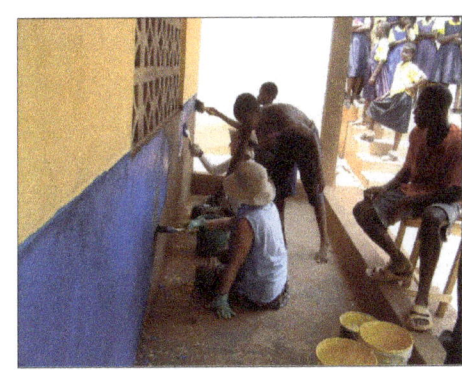
Team painting at the school

The whole team visited the Nsawan church for the Sunday morning service. Because of the problems with the previous injury, one team member felt that she could not go to the north where the roads were a lot worse, so she and another team member booked into a hotel on the ocean and the rest of the team left for the north, a fourteen-hour trip by car. We made a stop at Kintamp Falls with its one hundred fifty steps down and then the long one hundred fifty steps back up. The older I get, the harder it is. We then went on to Mole National Park, spent the night and went on safari early in the morning. We saw many wild animals, including elephants, then drove on to Tamale for a short stop, and then on to Salaga. The road remains in terrible shape. There is a new guest house, Timu Memorial Guest House, in Salaga and we got to stay there. A friend of Joe's who has cooked for Americans provided our main meal each night, a combination of Western and Ghanaian food, so the team got to taste the Ghanaian food.

Tuesday, April fifth we headed out for Buymondu where *PRO* is building a clinic, It was not finished so we held the clinic under the big mango tree and saw more than one hundred thirty-five people working for five-and-a-half hours, but couldn't see any more even though many others came. Aiden was doing first aid here, and there were so many infected sores that he ran out of supplies.

On April sixth, we drove to Kapiato and held a clinic from ten to one p.m. Joe and Jemima met with groups of people and pastors, including a group of twelve professionals who have converted from Islam. We attended

Lynn and Ruth doing a clinic at Kapiato

a service in Doganjida with Pastor Divine under a big mango tree and toured Sabonjida, seeing the new church building that was built on the foundation originally intended for a clinic. The government built a new clinic right near where we had started our clinic building and then told us we couldn't build a clinic there. There was a pastor's meeting where we learned about the great need for bicycles for pastors. We had extra money, so we bought four bicycles and twenty bags of cement for the Bukymondu clinic construction.

The water was high enough for us to take the ferry across Volta Lake, the area that was flooded for the construction of

Loaded ferry

the Volta River dam. This ferry cut off a lot of driving for our return trip to Tema, but it was a frightening experience with huge trucks and walk-on people sitting on top of the car part of the ferry. A young woman got on late with three babies, and there was no place for her to sit. No one gave her a seat so I got up and gave her mine—which made all the Ghanaians really look. After talking with her, she said that her sister had died in childbirth and there was no one to look after her triplets, so she was taking

Unloading vehicles and people from the heavily-loaded ferry

them home with her to raise them.

We were very tired by the time we made it back to Tema. Sunday we attended church at Ashainam. On Monday the tenth, we shopped at the carving village of Aburi and then made it back for Jemima's birthday party.

We had taken supplies to be donated to a hospital so, while we were doing our last minute shopping and getting our luggage checked in at the airport, Joe and Jemima took them to a psychiatric hospital to donate them, and spent some time singing and praying with the patients.

There was a long layover in Amsterdam, so we took the train into the city, walked around, and took a canal tour. It was quite cool after the Ghanaian warm temperatures. We made it safely back to the airport and off to Canada. Some of us took the airport bus back to Kingston, and some had family meeting them at the airport. It was disappointing to have to separate from the team like that, as I like to have a time of debriefing when everyone is back home.

Reflections by Lynn Rigby–2006 team
Memories of Ghana

- "The oppressive heat, the bustle of activity all night when the sun was down, when only the twenty-four-hour heat remained, and people were trying to get work done
- The village in the north where we did a clinic, and so many of the children were malnourished and terrified of the white 'ghosts'
- The rough roads to the game park which had no electricity and no water. The Jeep was broken, so we did a walking safari armed with one elephant gun.
- The eclipse of the sun!!!
- The slave trading post when felt so ashamed to be white
- The precious Ghanaian people who remain in my heart

- The wonderful church services with wonderful singing
- The wonderful members of our team
- My best friend, Ruth, my son, and dear Connie
- Joe and Jemina Ocran—gracious servants of the Lord
- Evelyn Sabbi, Pastor Gideon, and many other pastors

"The trip was definitely a quality experience for which I am grateful. Thank you for leading and sharing, Carole."

Chapter 21

The Second Dental Team 2007

With a dental team of seven planning to go to Northern Ghana, I knew there would be extra planning needed, so I went to Ghana ahead of the team. We left on June twenty-eighth, flying British Air this time. Because of delays at Heathrow, we were an hour late arriving in Ghana. Jemima had to wait two hours for me. Four medical students from Laval University in Quebec City had gone to Ghana earlier. I met with them, gave them the things I had brought from Canada for them, and got caught up on how things were going. Ghana Day is July first, the same as Canada Day, so it was a holiday weekend with celebrations, special games for both children and adults, and exciting things happening. I took first-aid supplies and treated twenty-five people at the soccer game competitions. Wesleyan Women won at the soccer competition and Wesleyan men won at the volleyball competition.

Evelyn, the Projects Officer for *Project Reach Out Ghana*, and I, visited the Ashiyie Community Clinic and the next day went to Anum School. We did some first-aid there, bought things to update their first-aid kit and donated the school supplies that I had brought from Canada. From there we drove on to Klefe Vocational School. We bought some fabric for the school sewing class to make things for me to take back to Canada to sell. The next day we went to the Ayikume farm, and on up the mountain to Aburi to shop for things for the Ghana Market in Canada.

It was the rainy season, so it rained three or four times a day. On Monday, July seventh I headed by State bus to Northern Ghana—a long, uncomfortable ride. I was staying at Akma guesthouse where I've stayed several times with Joe and other teams. Jemima was concerned about me being by myself and had Pastor Addison come to Tamale to escort me. I had to pay for his accommodation at the Akma, all his meals, expenses, and transportation—not an expense in my budget! I made reservations for the dental team at the Gariba Hotel (a beautiful five-star hotel) and arrangements for airport pick-up.

A pastor in Tamale was supposed to make contact with me about finding villages for the dental team to work in, but he hadn't made contact. I had left several messages for him, but he hadn't responded, so I decided to go to the Yendi district. Peter Jato, the district overseer for the Wesleyan church, came to Tamale to accompany me.

I was feeling some serious side-effects from the medication that I was taking to prevent malaria: terrible dreams, bouts of crying, and hallucinations. I woke myself up yelling, and when I asked Pastor Addison if he had heard me down the hall, he said he had.

Pastor Peter Jato and I went by taxi and drove to Bofoyili, taking the "short-cut." The road was absolutely terrible. *PROG* had started building a clinic there and arrangements were made for the dental team to go there. On the way back, the police stopped the taxi, and the driver was arrested for not having the proper license plates. I gave him some money so he could eat, and the police took Pastor Peter and me to the bus depot. A half-hour later, the taxi driver drove up. The police had taken his money as a bribe and let him go. He said they didn't want me, the white lady, to see them taking a bribe. When I had given the driver the money, I had told him that I would pray for him; because he was released, he said now I was his mother!

Peter Jato found Pastor Emmanuel, the Tamale pastor I had tried, unsuccessfully, for three days to contact. He finally came with Peter to talk to me. He talked a lot about "his NGO, his churches," and "his" everything. It seemed that he had some type of support from the United States as he had rented a six-bedroom house and had a new motorbike, a computer, and an office that was not being paid for by the Ghana mission. I made it very clear that I would be making the decisions for the dental team and his responsibility would be to find villages where they could work. He wanted money, but I was firm that I would not leave money for him or promise my help, and that the team would do only what we came to do—to see dental problems. He did not want Pastor Addison to be with me, but I insisted. I also insisted that he was not to talk to the dentists about money or support.

On Saturday, July fourteenth I hired a taxi and went to Salaga and then on to Bukyondu. The clinic building was complete, but there was no nurse. The government had taken over our property where the school had been, and built their own school—so much for using the site to build a church! We drove through the river to go to Wiae. They tied a plastic bag over the tailpipe and pushed

Stuck in the ditch

the taxi—with the driver and me in it—through the river with the water coming in around all the doors.

A crew of men dipped the water out of the taxi, and we went on our way to see the completed clinic. I visited with the chief and then was pushed back across the river with even more water coming into the car—and I have the video to prove it! On the way back, there was road construction. When the taxi driver tried to go around, the car went into the ditch. The construction crew had to come and pull us out with the big grader.

The new Wiae clinic ready to use

Back in Tamale, we had to try to deal with Pastor Emmanuel. After much praying on my part, he finally agreed to take me to see a chief after I actually started out walking to see him myself. The chief wanted us to come for three days of clinics. He had a building called a pavilion that would work as a site for the clinics. There was another village where we could go for another couple of days. The dental team arrived in Accra, and Pastor Emmanuel came on Monday to apologize for his actions the day before, and to ask to be included in the clinics. He wanted to go to the Gariba

Hotel and talk to the team; but I said no, he could not contact the team except at the clinics. I transferred to the Gariba Hotel. Evelyn and the van driver left Tema early with all the dental team's luggage and clinic supplies and arrived at the hotel late in the day. The Laval medical students had planned on traveling to the north for a holiday, so they came along in the van too.

We had shipped the dental supplies again for this team, and the shipment got there just in time for the team to arrive. This went on our list of miracles for this trip.

Monday, July sixteenth there were heavy, black storm clouds as I headed for the airport to meet the dental team. I prayed hard that the plane would land before the rains came and it did. Just as the team got into the terminal, the thunder, lightning and heavy rain started. When we were ready to pack everything into the Gariba transfer bus, the rain stopped, and we went to the hotel. The rain continued on and off the rest of the day. When it came time for us to walk to the dining room, the rain stopped.

Jeff Wahn, Linda Maloney, Linda Owen, Lawrence, Cindy and Alyssa Reimer, Barb and Ian Wahn, and myself

Tuesday morning we went to the village of Kapa-Ylii and set up. We were greeted by the chief and the elders, but this being a Muslim village, our having a female as leader was not received well. There were some restrictions. Barb Wahn, the female dentist, could not treat the men, and the children would have to wait until all the men were attended to. We prayed and started for the day. The Laval students showed up to help, and I sent them to the area schools to do some first aid and give out deworming medicine and chewable vitamins to as many children as they could find. They estimated that they saw about four hundred fifty kids. The dentists set up with Lawrence treating the men; Barb treating the women; Ian doing the sterilization of instruments; Linda doing plaque removal; and Alyssa, Jeff and our other Linda assisting the dentists. Cindy manned the medication table, and I did triage with all the people waiting in line to be seen—treating eye and ear infections, skin problems, coughs, arthritic type pain, and babies with diarrhea. I don't know how many people we actually saw, but it was many! We were all tired.

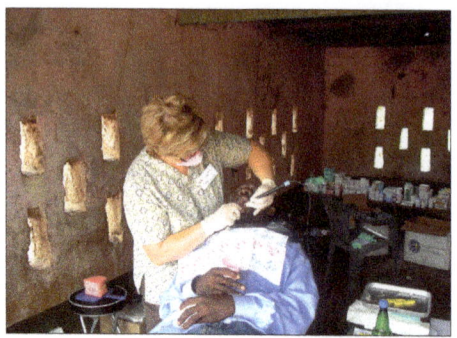

Linda O. de-scaling

The pavilion where we set up to work

We returned to the hotel for debriefing, food, Bible study, and prayer. The temperature was thirty-six Celsius. Heavy rain in the night with the power off meant no air-conditioning, and it was hot and humid. However, altogether it was a good, productive day.

July eighteenth, we went back to the same village where the power had been off. Linda's Cavitron was set up with a gas generator. Later, when the power came back on, someone plugged it directly into the two-twenty power and blew the unit,

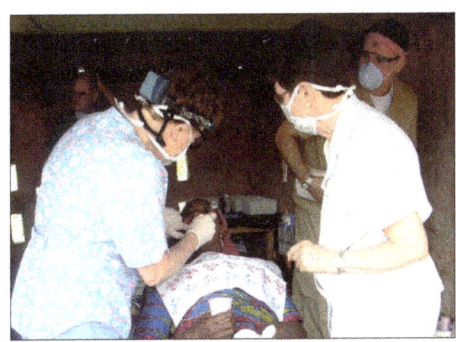

Barb pulling teeth

so she had to go back to manual scaling.

Evelyn and I went into the city to buy some more medications, and the driver took the rented bus to a mechanic. It turned out we, not the company who owned the bus, had to pay for

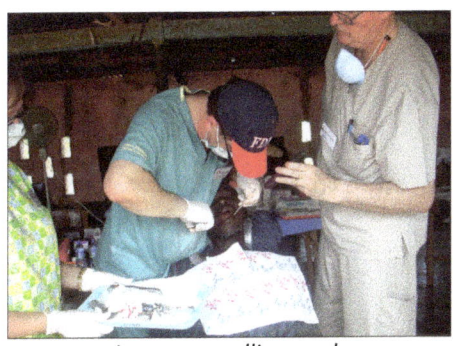

Lawrence pulling teeth

the repairs. While we were gone, a news team from the television station came and interviewed the dentists. We continued our work, and Linda O. and Alyssa gave lessons in brushing and flossing. Everyone was pushing and shoving trying to get free toothbrushes.

All the instruments ready to use

Carole seeing as many people as possible

I found Pastor Emmanuel visiting the dentists in their room. I didn't ask him why he was there, since he knew I had asked him not to go there. The last day of the clinic at the chief's palace in Tamale, the elders came to me, saying the chief wanted to see me. My mind conjured up all kinds of scenarios. Had we done something wrong? Had we offended someone? Was he upset with me, a female, as the leader of the group? When I entered his palace, he was sitting on a large cowhide against a wall. I was expected to sit on the floor, but I said I couldn't get down there or get up again. They brought a small stool for me to sit on. Normally, the chief does not speak directly to a visitor, but speaks through a linguist. As soon as the linguist started to speak, the chief said in English, "I wish to speak for myself." He asked me why we had come and why we didn't ask for his people to pay for their care. He couldn't understand why professionals would leave their practices, travel all the way to Ghana without pay, pay their own expenses, and treat his people without charge. I explained that we loved God, and He loved us, and that God also loved him and his people. I explained

Waiting line at Kpanvo clinic

how it is our responsibility, as Christians, to show God's love by helping those in need. That was why we had come. He pondered for quite a while before speaking the words that have become the title for this book: "*Words Fail Me.*"

Giving school supplies to the Kpanvo school

Thursday and Friday we were off to the village of Kpanvo for two days of clinics. We had a proper building—a clinic with rooms where we could work. There were so many people at the village that we had to close the gates and let in new people when the ones we had treated left. I was able to go to the local school and donate school supplies and sports equipment. The teacher at this school told me quietly that he was the only Christian in the entire Muslim village.

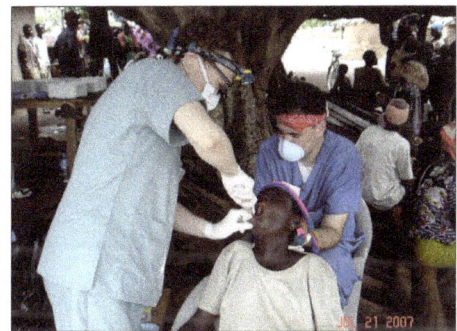
Dr. Barbara working under a tree with Jeff holding the patients heads during treatment

When we got back to the hotel, I told the team that I was not feeling well. I had a temperature of thirty-eight-point-six Celsius. So the team went back to the village without me. I spent a terrible night. My temp was one hundred two-point-one Fahrenheit in the morning, and I had a really congested chest.

It was Joe's birthday, so we called him and all sang "Happy Birthday." Because of my condition, it was decided that I should stay at the hotel, and the team would go on to the village of Bofoyili for the day.

River crossing to Boyoyili

In order to get to the village, the bus had to drive through the river. Fortunately, the water was low enough that they could drive through. However, there was no place for the team to work, so someone held the patient's head while sitting on a chair, and they worked under trees. Cindy was able to treat children with worm medicine and vitamins. There was a long line of people waiting to be treated.

Monday, July twenty-third the team, minus Linda O. and me (who were both sick), went back to the village of Kpanvo. People started queuing up at four a.m. Cindy, with help from Pastor Emmanuel, dispensed medications, and the dentists saw thirty-three dental patients. Many more were seen with medical complaints. Tuesday we all went back to Kpanvo. The dentists saw twenty-five to thirty patients, and we treated approximately

Line to receive worm medicine

two hundred medical patients. We thanked all the volunteers and gave them a stipend. Pastor Emmanuel ended up being a big help with the clinics. We packed up everything in the bus, ready for their trip back to Tema in the morning.

Wednesday, July twenty-fifth we checked out of the hotel and went to the airport. We endured a very slow and thorough search of luggage, and body searches of people, before we flew back to Accra to stay in the Mensvic Hotel. Thursday we shopped for souvenirs and took the remainder of the medications to Jemima for the Ashiyie Clinic. We had a celebratory dinner with gifts for Joe's birthday.

Friday, July twenty-seventh we packed up, signed out of the hotel and went on a tour of the city of Accra. It was the fiftieth anniversary of independence, and everything was painted up and clean. The African Unity Conference was being held in Ghana. We checked in at the airport and then went for supper at the Landing Restaurant with Joe, Jemima, and Evelyn. Our flight to Heathrow was good. Cindy, Alyssa, and Linda O. took the "tube" into Piccadilly Circus while the rest of us rested at the airport.

On the flight to Montreal, I was able to do all the paperwork for the Ghana Market purchases for Customs. We landed and cleared Customs with no problems. My cold was still bothersome with a lot of coughing. I ended up going to the doctor when I got home and was diagnosed with a form of Legionnaires disease, an infection from air conditioning units that had not been properly cleaned and sanitized. Two rounds of antibiotics made me as good as new again.

Despite many hurdles, we again had a successful team trip. Only God can take all the problems and make them into a memorable experience.

Reflections from Alyssa Reimer:

Alyssa Reimer, a sixteen-year-old member of our team wrote the following note: "This trip in 2007 was a significant life event for me, as I came home with a different attitude and approach to life. It felt like a big adjustment at sixteen-years-old. I credit my parents for bringing me along, and exposing me to the painful realities of a developing country. I plan to do the same thing with my teenagers one day. Thanks to all for contributing to such a special life-altering event for me, even if it didn't feel that way at the time."

Reflections from Linda Owen PRO Dental Mission Team–2007

"In July, 2007, I was fortunate once again to be included in *Project Reach Out*'s dental mission to Ghana, specifically in the northern region of Tamale.

"Our first clinic days took place in a village area we were told was primarily of Muslim faith. Our goal was not only to provide much needed dental treatment and pain relief, but to show Christ's love through action and compassion. Each morning at the "Chief's Palace," we joined hands and sang praises to God in view of the growing lineup of patients seeking care. Our clinic site here was literally three block walls and a concrete floor with no electricity at all; certainly not the palatial conditions I had envisioned prior to arrival!

"As a dental hygienist, I saw that, while oral needs were significant, they were really quite secondary in light of overall medical problems of many who sought treatment. As a mother, I could empathize with the unwavering determination of many women pushing for a place in line, desperate for their children to receive dental cleaning, a toothbrush, floss, and toothpaste for their home care. The dentists did an amazing job providing extractions, antibiotics, and post-operative instruction; exhibiting love, and a spirit of care, despite tough working conditions.

"A highlight for our team was having two opportunities to experience Ghanaian Christian worship, both in Tamale region and near Accra. I was personally overwhelmed with the authenticity and joyful spirit of praise in their churches, particularly through song and dance!

"Upon my return to Canada, I was frequently asked how this experience impacted my life. Frankly, I feel that we were the ones who came away blessed beyond measure. I wish that I could have done more. We take so much for granted and too often aren't truly thankful for what we have in our culture. I will always be grateful to God for the opportunity to have been a part of this experience in Ghana."

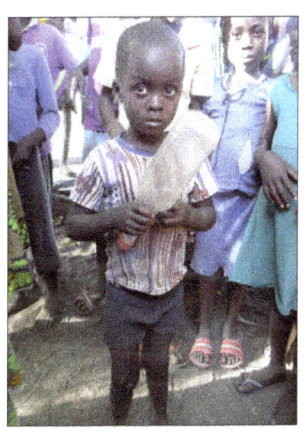

*Joe and Jemima Ocran,
Darrell and Debbie Lamos and myself*

Chapter 22

Visitors and Conference–2009

My mother gave me the gift of a limousine ride to Dorval airport, so David Brown and his special service came and picked me up on Thursday, November nineteenth, 2009. It was cold and rainy in Amsterdam, but not in Ghana! Darrell and Debbie Lamos had taken a year off their pastoral ministry to live in Ghana and assist Joe Ocran with the work of the mission. They had rented a beautiful house and I was able to stay with them until their daughter arrived to visit for American Thanksgiving.

I spent a restful weekend doing a bit of shopping, unpacking and going to church.

Everyone was busy getting ready for the biannual church conference. Church officials from South Africa and the United States were coming in to attend. I was able to visit Ashiyie Community Clinic, where staff were almost all new, and went on to Ayikumc farm. The government had cancelled the seedling contracts. This had been a profitable contract for our farm to supply tree seedlings for the government's reforestation of the riverbanks. However, when the new government was elected, it cancelled all the programs that had been begun by the defeated government, and our seedling program was one of them. The farm grows okra, red peppers, mango, and pineapple to sell. We went on to the Ashalley-Botwe Kinder Care

School and saw forty-five children, ages three to six. We then spent some time with Jemima making up kits for the pastors' wives. We decided to give each pastor's wife (or if he was unmarried, his mother) a four-yard piece of Ghanaian cloth at the conference.

Wednesday I headed off with Evelyn, the Projects Officer for *Project Reach Out Ghana*, to the Anum School. They now had electricity and were able to start computer classes. The government had a new policy that every student graduating from Junior Secondary School, grade nine, must know how to use a computer. We gave out supplies and library books that we had brought from Canada. Then we proceeded to Klefe Vocational School near the city of Ho. The second building was under construction. This building was being funded partially by the memorials from my husband Lorne's funeral.

Mixing cement by hand at the Klefe Vocational School construction site

We were able to give six students sewing machines on their graduation from the program. Fifty-six seedling mango trees from our Ayikume farm have been taken to Klefe and planted there for some income generation. The conference started on Friday, November twenty-seventh and I gave a report on the work of *Project Reach Out Canada* in partnership with *Project Reach Out Ghana*. Zach Szmara arrived from the U.S. and stayed with Darrell and Debbie as well. He was looking at Ghana as a potential missionary experience for himself and his family. After conference was finished, Darrell and Debbie's daughter arrived and I moved to Joe and Jemima's guest room.

Wednesday, December second Zach, Evelyn, the driver, Nana, and I left for Northern Ghana. We stopped at Kintempo Falls then drove on to Tamale. Thursday, after talking to the staff at the Tamale Nursing College Government Hospital about potential nursing scholarships, we left and took the "shake, rattle, and roll" road to Salaga. We checked in to the Maridon Lodge Guest House, and the air conditioning worked. Evelyn and I had planned the trip and where we would visit, but Zach was interested in the churches more than the *PRO* projects, so we had to adjust things.

Friday we visited the church leaders at Loloto, Sabonjida, and Kabeso. The clinic at Kabeso needed a nurse and I had been investigating the possibility of going there for six months or so, until one of the three-year nursing scholarship students would graduate and could take over. We considered all the necessities for me to live there:

The ferry at Makngo taking off for Yeji

The well at Kekpeni dug for PRO

housing, transportation, food, water, health care, professional nursing work and how it would be carried out, protection, safety et cetera. We went to visit the chief to get his ideas and permission. The only obstacle was the fact that I still looked after my mother, who was ninety-two years old at the time. I wouldn't be able to do this until she is no longer living, so everything had to be put on hold. The chief asked, "Should I pray for a long life for your mother or an early death?" No promises were made. God had a plan and we would let Him work out the details.

We went on to Kakpeni to see the borehole (well) that was drilled with the donations of the friends of Caitlan Freeman, the CIDA Youth Intern working with us that year.

We started the trip back to the South by taking the ferry from Makango to Yeji, across a part of Lake Volta that was flooded when they put in the Akosombo dam. There were still trees sticking out of the water and other things that made us follow the sign on a truck we could see on the ferry. It said, "Let us pray," and we did—long and hard! The ferry was overloaded, and not to the standards of the West, but we made it safely. It was eleven p.m. by the time we got back to Tema. I was very tired and tripped on a cord strung across the room and fell, hurting both my knees. So that night I went to bed with ice on my knees.

Sunday, December sixth Zach, Darrell and Debbie went off to preach at Tema New Town Church ,and I went with Joe and Jemima to fundraising Sunday at Ashiaman. The internet was working, so I was able to catch an e-mail from home to discover that my niece had had a baby girl.

Monday, I visited the West African AIDS Foundation (WAAF) clinic Out Patients department. Most of the hospitals in Accra refer all their HIV positive patients to WAAF. Besides treating the patients, they have a "Sponsor An Orphan" program. They concentrate on the education of children with HIV. The HIV/AIDS incidence is much lower in Ghana than in other African countries. There was heavy rain today, but the temperature remained at plus thirty, so it was very uncomfortable with the humidity. We did some shopping for the Ghana Market at home.

Early on Tuesday morning Joe, Evelyn, and I left for New Edubiase, Joe's home town, where *PRO* had started building a vocational school that would be a combination of a computer lab and a reading library. The property is on the grounds of a huge school complex which accommodates crèche or nursery school through primary school (kindergarten through grade six), Junior Secondary School (which is grades seven to nine), and Senior Secondary School (grades ten

Start of the construction of the building at New Edubiase.

to twelve). In total, there were well over 1,000 students. There was no library and there were no computers at this time in these schools. The original $10,000 from Canada would build the building and the roof, but would not fund the cement pad for the floor, the electricity, the septic tank, internet connections, toilets, or any of the furnishings. It would take a lot more money to finish it.

We visited Joe's sister's restaurant for lunch, and then went to visit the chief, Joe's cousin, before heading back home. It was over thirty-two degrees Celsius in my room, and I had only a fan for relief. We spent Wednesday getting things ready to start for home and doing the last-minute shopping for the Ghana Market. In the evening, there was a huge storm. Temperatures rose to over thirty-seven, celsius, before the storm. Not surprisingly, the power went off during and after the storm.

Thursday, December seventh we shopped for NIV Bibles for the pastors, and were able to find some in Accra. I bought a set of tapes on learning the Twi language, but with my history of poor marks in all languages, I didn't hold out much hope of actually learning to speak it. I have learned a few words but not enough! We headed for the airport. My leg was really bothering me, so I was able to get early boarding assistance—much to the agitation of some Ghanaians awaiting regular boarding. When we got to Amsterdam, I found my way to the "comfort" chairs and was able to doze off. On the flight to Canada, I did all my accounting for the trip, wrote part of the *PRO* newsletter, and started my report to the *PRO Canada* board. When I arrived in Montreal, there was Dave Brown with my winter coat and the limousine ride back to Brockville. Oh such comfort; a smooth road, even though it was snowing, a warm coat, and time to close my eyes and sleep. It was a rush again to get ready for Christmas, but it had been worth it all. Thank you Lord for another safe trip.

Chapter 23

Here–Take My Child

During my working experience in Canada, I met a Ghanaian student nurse by the name of Dankwa. He and his wife were living in Brockville while he was going through nurses training. He had come to Canada, asked for political asylum and ended up in Brockville, where he was being sponsored by a program through Unemployment Insurance to provide vocational training. He was having difficulty with racial prejudice in the almost one hundred percent white population in Brockville. Understanding some of his Ghanaian customs, I decided to befriend him and his wife, and help them deal with the prejudice they were encountering. They were a unique couple. They became a part of our church family. Dankwa's wife, Vida, helped us with the food for a fundraising Ghanaian dinner sponsored by *Project Reach Out Canada.*

During the time that we were acquainted, they had marital problems, and Dankwa wrote to his mother that he wanted a divorce from his wife. His mother replied that the families had met and that their tribal marriage contract had been revoked. He was now divorced, according to the Ghanaian tradition of marriage and divorce customs. Vida left Brockville, and I didn't see either of them again until I was at the airport in Ghana returning from a team trip.

I heard children calling "Auntie Carole, Auntie Carole" and there, coming towards me, was Vida with two children; a boy and a girl, with suitcases. It turned out that Vida had returned to Ghana and was working at the airport. She knew that I was visiting Ghana. She had brought her children for me to "take" them to Canada so they could be with her former husband. I had had no warning—no one had asked me beforehand, and now I had these two children hanging on to my clothes and crying, assuming that I would take them to Canada. There were no Visas and no plane tickets. I was flabbergasted! Of course I refused to take them. They were very insistent, with much crying. All I could see in my mind's eye was Ghanaian newspaper headlines, "Canadian Missionary Kidnaps Ghanaian Children."

I quickly went through Customs and left them behind, never to be heard from again. I later heard that Dankwa had graduated and gotten a position as a nurse in Texas. Apparently, he later became a head nurse and was very successful.

Chapter 24

Hurry up and Wait!
2011

September twenty-third, 2011, I took off for Ghana by myself. I drove to Toronto and left my car at the Carlingview Hotel near the airport. In a previous chapter, I said that if ever I needed a hotel in Toronto, I would stay at the Carlingview. Because I had registered a reservation to stay there upon my return from Ghana, I was able to leave my car in the parking lot, free of charge. The trip to Ghana through Amsterdam was uneventful, even though the Toronto leg was late taking off and arriving in Amsterdam.

Joe and Jemima were there to meet me and take me to the D. B. Lodge guesthouse in Sakumono. Their logo is, "Where Every Guest is Treated As a Royal." Not quite true, but the place was neat and clean. I cooked my own meals, so I had to shop right away. The water was off for a whole day and the internet not working. I was able to borrow a phone and eventually buy my own, so I called home to let them know I had arrived safely.

It was different being by myself with no one to talk to. A student nurse living in the same building helped me a bit with trying to use the cook stove and facilities. I spent a lot of time waiting for people to come and take me places. The first few days, I visited the projects: Ashiyie community clinic, a well-baby clinic (being held under the new health care scheme despite the fact that there were still quite a few private paying patients), and the Ayikuma Farm. The pineapples had been harvested for sale and they were raising Grass Cutters (a rodent much like a ground hog that people eat). I went to the Ashalley-Botwe Kinder Care School and found that only thirty-five students were enrolled that year. They were feeding all students their noon meal at a cost of over one dollar U.S. per day. Then I went to the Wesleyan Academy Anum School where they had two hundred ninety students registered that year, with only thirteen teachers and the principal. They were also feeding their kindergarten students a noon meal. At the Klefe Vocational School, the second building was almost finished, and they were almost ready to start the floor. Once it was finished, they could apply to the National Vocational Training Institute for accreditation. Ashalley-Botwe church had moved to their own property, but the building had barely started. They had to carry all the furnishings to storage before and after every service. There was the most amazing little boy drummer at the church. His name was "Wonder."

This trip, I made arrangements for the first time to visit my *Compassion Canada* sponsored child, and also the *Compassion*

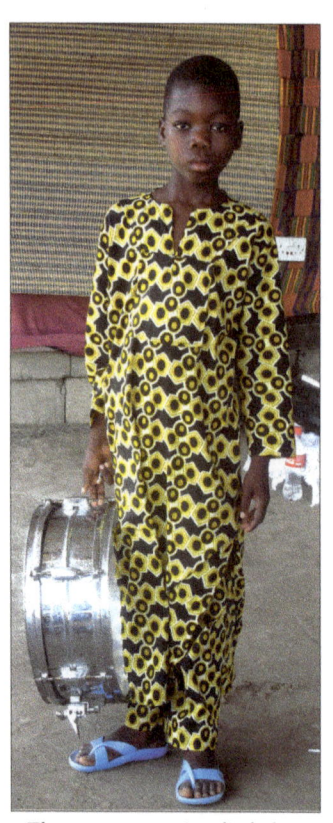

The most amazing little boy drummer, named "Wonder"

Canada child sponsored by the Children's ministry of Centennial Road Church. Monday, September twenty-sixth, we made the trip to Breman Jamra to visit my child, Ernestina. She was ten-years-old and very shy. No one had ever visited a sponsored child in this village, so everyone in the village showed up to see me. I gave gifts to her and to her grandparents with whom she lives, and saw her

Ernestina with me

home. We also visited with the *Compassion* staff and got an idea of what they do and how they do it. It was a long trip, but worth the effort.

On Wednesday the twenty-eighth, we made the trip to Accra to visit Rejoice, the church's sponsored child. She and her mother, two sisters and a brother, live in one room of a family compound in a very poor neighbourhood. A *Compassion* worker accompanied me. We gave gifts to Rejoice and her family.

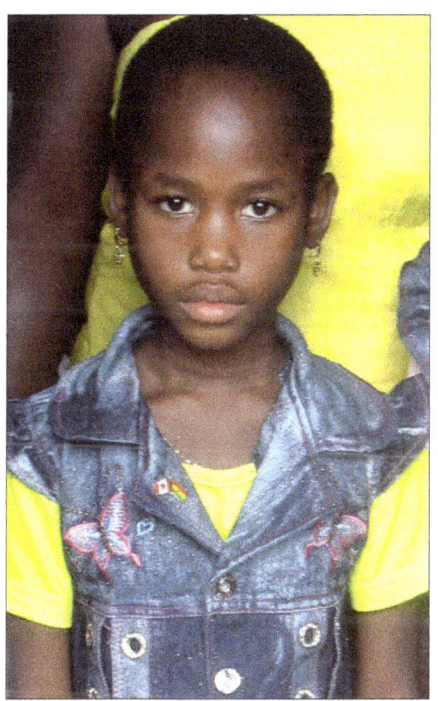

Rejoice, Compassion Canada child sponsored by the Centennial Road Church in Brockville, Ontario

The guesthouse where I was staying was full of Nigerians who were there for a wedding; so there was lots of noise, drinking, and partying. One big man came to my door and wanted to "get to know me better." I ended up closing the door firmly in his face.

On Sunday, Diella worked on my phone trying to get it to charge properly. My Cogeco account wouldn't work at all, so she set up a G-mail account for me that finally worked.

I took a taxi into Tema Community One to shop for the Ghana Market in Canada. *Project Reach Out Ghana* board met to consider the revisions to the constitution, offering some suggestions. There was so much going on with the church that there was no time to do the things that needed to be done. I was thankful that I had brought my Kindle, which enabled me to read a lot. I had brought Christmas gifts for the Ocrans, so I was able to take the time to wrap them properly.

The best Chinese food I have ever eaten was in Ghana. Every trip there, I take the Ocrans out for a Chinese meal, and this time was no exception. It was so good, but each year the prices increase.

On Tuesday, October eleventh, Joe and I picked up his friend Baffour and drove to Northern Ghana. Baffour is the Dean of Theology at All Nations University in Korfoidua. It is not a trip to the north without at least one flat tire. This trip it was two, so we had to stop in Techiman to make repairs and buy two used tires. It took so long that we had to stay there overnight. We were traveling in the original mobile clinic van. It was on its third motor and had serious mechanical problems and the air-conditioning didn't work.

We drove straight through to Wa in the very northwest of Ghana, where we met Pastor Ossman. We visited a church site and a school and met with church members. We also went to a couple of villages where churches have been planted. I can't use the names of the villages because there could be Muslim backlash against the church members. We drove all the way back to Techiman and then turned north again for Tamale—ten-and-a-half hours of driving. We stayed at Redach Hotel for one night and then went on to Salaga over the terrible 'shake, rattle and roll' road. We stayed at the Maridon Lodge again; unfortunately, it was very dirty this time. We had to spray and clean before we could move in.

Following a pastors' meeting, our driver, Eric, took me to Upando to see the new church there. We all went to Kabeso, but the clinic was closed. The *PRO* sign was gone, and a Ghana Health Services sign was in its place. Joe preached and then listened to all the problems. The people gave us a goat (which I named Sheldon) as a gift. Then back to Salaga and on to Tamale over the terrible road again. It rained very hard, and the van leaked—so when we got to Redach, I was wet and covered with red mud. I really enjoyed the shower, with the first hot water in a while.

Nandundo— approximately two hundred people were waiting under a tree for the service

On Sunday, we drove to Yendi and picked up Pastor Philip for the first service in the village of Nandundo. There were about two hundred people with over one hundred children waiting under a tree for the service. It took two pictures to get everyone in the photo.

A twenty-one-year-old young man, John, a senior in high school, was there. He had been a Christian for four years and will pastor this church. This village is the home village of Pastor Isaac, the district pastor, who started the church. Before we left, the church gave us a chicken (which I named Destiny) because its destiny was the cooking pot!

When it was time to go, we had trouble starting the van. It frequently sputtered along the way. We had to be pushed to get started many times. In total, we traveled seven hours! We were very tired and dirty.

Monday, October seventeenth at five-thirty a.m., we headed back to the south, traveling a total of twelve hours. We spent a couple of days shopping for the Ghana Market and visiting back at the clinic and Ashalley-Botwe school; and then on Wednesday the nineteenth, we went to New Edubaise. Building for the vocational school had not progressed much from where it had been two years previously, because there was no money to finish it.

Thursday, October twentieth was head-for home day. I visited with Margaret Caesar, a *PROG* board member. She was so excited that her first grandchild had been born, and was planning to go to England to see her. A couple of weeks after I got home, Joe phoned to say that Margaret had died and never got to see her granddaughter. So sad! She was such a lovely woman, and had worked hard to make a life in Ghana with her Ghanaian husband and two sons. We left for the airport and made it through Customs and Immigration with no problems. We did a bit of Christmas shopping in Schiphol airport in Amsterdam and had a good flight to Toronto.

When I arrived in Toronto, I was picked up by the Carlingview transfer car, and they told me that they had upgraded my room. It was a beautiful suite with a Jacuzzi tub and living room and a king-sized bed. What a luxury! Wesley and Sonia, my son and daughter-in-law, came to have dinner with me at a lovely restaurant in the hotel. I was craving salad and they brought me a gorgeous one! I don't eat salads in Ghana unless Jemima makes them. There is too much possibility of contaminated raw vegetables being used. I had a good night's sleep, and drove back to Brockville the next day. Safely home, I reevaluated future trips as I had spent more money than I planned, and had spent a lot of time alone and waiting on people.

Atop the safari jeep

Chapter 25

Ghana and Burkina Faso 2014 Team

Three people make up this year's team: Elizabeth Sue-Ann Smith (Liz to me, Beth to her family), her sister Jane Burgess, and I. A different airline connection this time too: Air Canada to Toronto and Air Lufthansa to Frankfurt and on to Ghana.

One thing I have insisted on when labeling luggage, is that Joe Ocran's phone number is included on the luggage tag. This trip that detail was a God-send, as Liz picked up a suitcase that was identical to hers, right down to

Carole, Liz, and Jane at Ashalley-Botwe church

the Air Canada luggage tag. We were packing all the luggage in Joe's vehicle when his phone rang, saying that Customs had a piece of red luggage with his phone number, and the luggage did not belong to the person who had retrieved it. It turned out that the bag Liz had picked up was not hers, so...back into the airport to find the person who had her bag. We stayed at the Chesterfield Hotel in Sakumono. Sunday, March twenty third we attended the Ashalley-Botwe Wesleyan Church. They gave me a new Ghanaian name: "Ewura Abena." I know the Abena means, "Tuesday-born female."

Jane is a birder, someone who watches, identifies, and catalogs birds. She was excited to see what species she could find in Ghana and Burkina Faso that are different from the many other countries she has visited.

The first few days were spent visiting the *Project Reach Out* projects and cataloging everything for the reports I prepare for the *Project Reach Out Canada* board on the Ashiyie Community Clinic, the Ayikuma farm, the Anum school (Wesleyan Academy), and Klefe Vocational School when I get home. The bridge over the Volta River was still under repair, so we had to take the ferry—always an interesting time! We also shopped for things to take back to sell in our Ghana Market. On Thursday we drove to Cape Coast and Elmina where, the following day, we took a tour of the Slave Castle at Elmina and then drove back to Accra and Tema.

Friday, March twenty eighth we packed up and left the Chesterfield Hotel at five a.m. We headed north, accompanied by Faustina Yalley, Joe's secretary, and Pastor Kwame Frempong. Liz has a medical condition that requires lots of rest, so she slept almost all the way—awake only for pit stops and to eat. We took a detour to go to the Mole National Park, an elephant refuge. Early the next morning, we climbed onto the park Jeep and took the two-hour tour seeing warthogs, antelope, monkeys, elephants, and all kinds of birds—which made Jane really happy.

We had just gotten out on the road when we came across a camel caravan, something I had never seen before in Ghana.

In Tamale, we stayed at Redach Hotel, very tired and ready for sleep. I slipped getting into the tub and cut myself on the wood surrounding the tub. Sunday morning we headed out for the Yendi district to church at Kambordo. Pastor Kwame preached and, following the service, we held a clinic where we registered one hundred eleven people—but were unable to see everyone. A storm was coming, and we didn't want to get stuck in the mud in this village. We were able to have Dawuni with us, a very talented physician's assistant from Yendi hospital who speaks twelve languages and dialects. Joe flew from Accra to join us.

Because of the rain, we couldn't go to the next planned village so we did paper work, went to the market, and went to an Arts Centre with local crafts in Tamale—all the way ducking in and out of the rain and straddling puddles. Because the rains caused muddy conditions in the villages, arrangements were made for us to hold a clinic on Tuesday in a suburb of Tamale called Vitten, a totally Muslim sector. Clinic lasted from nine-fifteen a.m. to four p.m., with only a fifteen-minute lunch break—with the inevitable "men have to be seen first" scenario of a Muslim village. The chief came in all his finery to observe our work.

We were all very tired at the end of the day. On Wednesday, Liz stayed at the hotel, and the rest of the team headed for the small village of Katinguli, which had a total of sixty-three houses. Pastor Philip was the pastor of this church of twenty adults and many children. We saw ninety-six people. The chief sent his emissaries to offer me a marriage proposal. He offered seven cows for me but I politely declined his proposal.

The "man of my dreams" – the chief – offers a marriage proposal!

When we got back to the hotel, our first nursing scholarship student to graduate from nursing college arrived to meet us. He was doing his required national service before starting his nursing career.

Nursing scholarship student Ibrahim with Joe and Carole

Thursday, April third we packed up the car and headed north through Bolgatanga and into Burkina Faso, arriving in Ouagadougaou at five-fifteen p.m. Pastor Theophlllis met us for supper, and then we went to the guesthouse. The power was off, so we had no air-conditioning, no fans, no wifi or internet—and to top it all off—no water! We used bottled water to wash up and were too tired to do anything, even unpack. They finally got a generator going, and we had fans by bedtime. The refrigerators weren't working because of the power outage, so we had to throw away a lot of our food. There were no fridges in the rooms. The guesthouse had beautiful grounds, very lush with plants and flowers, and lots of birds—to Jane's delight. A wedding reception was being held there in the afternoon.

Friday we set off to register with the Health Department for the clinics. Because *Project Reach Out* is not known in Burkina Faso, we had all the bureaucratic mumbo jumbo to go through, and they wouldn't let us do the first clinic that was planned. They needed my work visa credentials—a country with some of the poorest health care in the world and they wouldn't let us help their people because I didn't have the credentials they thought I should have. I had to write a list of all my education, places I had worked with references et cetera—and they wanted a man to talk as the leader, even though Pastor Theo had previously made arrangements.

Saturday, we had clearance to do a clinic, so we went to the village of Kobua where we treated a hundred and three people under a tree, with a temperature of forty-one Celsius. Fortunately, there was a slight breeze. We encountered many of the same conditions as we had seen in Ghana.

R. Balkuy church – We held a clinic here

Structure where we held the clinic

One woman arrived in a trailer behind a motorcycle. She was very sick, and had had a stroke; we prayed with her and gave her a prayer shawl that we had brought from Canada. Sunday we attended church back at the village of Kobua, where they have an actual church building. We then went to the church at Balkuy to hold a clinic in the building. We treated a hundred twenty-seven people. We were so tired, and with the heat, it was hard to even eat a meal. Monday we packed everything, left the guesthouse and drove to Tanghir. We were stopped several times by the police for license checks.

We went on to Pastor Elizabeth's house, a two-room mud hut with no electricity or water. She had just had her fifth baby two days previously. All seven people lived in the hut. A clinic was organized in the bamboo and thatch church structure. We were able to treat only fifty-two people, as we had to leave to catch our flight to start our trip home. We left all

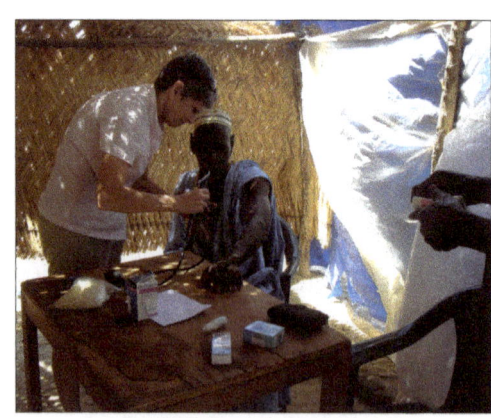
Jane assisting at the Tanghir clinic

the medicines with Pastor Theo and the physician's assistant with whom we were working. They went the day after we left to a village near the border with Ghana and treated over one hundred more people. Joe and the rest of the team returned to Ghana.

We left for the airport, stopping for supper and catching our overnight Brussels Airway flight to Belgium. When we left Burkina Faso, it was over forty degrees Celsius; in contrast, Belgium was only around ten degrees Celsius. From desert to lush vegetation, from sweating to shivering, from poverty to luxury. It was early morning when we arrived in Brussels, and our hotel was not ready until the afternoon; so we walked around the streets, had breakfast, booked a tour for the next day; and then, when the hotel room became available, we went to bed and slept for a few hours. After a really good and expensive supper, we had a debriefing time, sent e-mails to our families at home, and slept all night. The next day, we went enjoyed being tourists on a bus tour of Brussels. Thursday, April tenth we took a taxi to the airport at six forty-five a.m. for an Air France flight to Toronto. A fidgety woman sitting beside me pulled her carryon bag from the overhead bin and hit Liz on the

Liz Smith, Carole and Jane Burgess in Brussels

head, knocking her glasses off and her hearing aids out of her ears. Liz ended up with a lump on her forehead. The woman didn't even apologize. We took a commuter flight from Toronto to Ottawa, which arrived late, and Don and Betty Weatherhead picked Liz and me up. Jane's husband was there, as Ottawa is her home. Good to be home! Thank you, God, for a safe trip.

Team member reflection – Liz (Beth) Smith:

"I think that foremost in my mind was how hot it was there and how poor the people were. I had only seen villages like the ones we visited in books and magazines like National Geographic. Also, how polite the people were. At first I thought we were just doing "Band-Aid" help, but decided that a little help was better than no help at all.

"I was blown away with the landscape being so brown. I remember when we got to Brussels, the green of the landscape seemed so brilliant. It really was not, but after almost three weeks of all brown, that was the way it seemed to me.

"I am so glad that I went as I look at the world so differently now. Here we have everything, and I think that most people take that for granted; but after being there, I thank the Lord that I was born here—and I definitely do not take what we have for granted. It was quite an eye-opener for me. I was very thankful that I was able to go and do my very small part in helping these people. I wear the necklace that one of the ladies took off her own neck and put on mine. I was blown away about that.

"I am glad we got to go to Burkino Faso. I remember the extreme heat. I really do not know how you have done it for so many years."

Jane Burgess Reflections:

"I remember:

- being worried I would not know what to do once I got to Ghana. You said, 'Don't worry; you will find your place,' and Carole, you were so right. I am so thankful you included me. When we got there, it was so easy to go through because the security people knew Rev. Joe.

- being amazed at all the people who came to the clinics, especially on the day we had to leave early because of the rain. A whole group of people walked about twenty-five kilometres, just to attend the clinic. You had to decide who was going to be checked out by the nurse. I remember being so emotional about leaving a whole lot of people not looked after.

- going to the Muslim clinic and being so mindful of keeping their skin covered when I put on the blood pressure cuff—completely forgetting I was wearing capris.

- going to an outside restaurant and seeing all those huge fruit bats

- the elephant reserve—going up onto the top of the truck to sit so we could see all the birds and animals. I can still see you and Beth in my mind's eye climbing up and over the rail to get to your seats.

- going to the first school and being impressed with the education the kids were getting in such a rudimentary settling. It reminded me a bit of Upper Canada Village.

- the smiles on the children's faces when we gave them our

books for the school. I showed pictures of this to my own grandchildren, and won't forget the smiles on their faces knowing their own books were in Ghana, and that kids were learning from them.

- and who can forget your proposal, and how you diplomatically said 'no?'
- the church services were amazing. The congregation threw themselves into worship; it was clear to me they had a deep faith.
- Burkino Faso and the doctor who was so surprised when I told him his next patient was outside and I thought she had had a stroke. He said *he* was the doctor. When he came back, he said, 'How did you know she had a stroke?' He was amazed when I told him most people in Canada know the signs of stroke and heart attack.

"Thank you for letting me go with you to Ghana; it is a trip I shall never, never forget. On the spiritual side, you encouraged me to make a decision on my church-going habits. The Sunday after returning, I went to the United Church and have not left it."

Chapter 26

A Male-Dominated Team
2015

Lots of adventures. Stuck in the mud.

This was different. This was the first time I had been just a member of the team, rather than the leader in planning and executing the team visit to Ghana. I was part of the missions construction team for a Salaga guesthouse, even though I wouldn't be physically working on the guesthouse.

It started out that I would travel with five men and, on my own, I'd visit places in the north where I had taken teams in the past. About two months before we left, Kathy deSouza asked me who was going to Ghana. When she discovered I was going with five men, she said, "You are not going to Ghana alone with five guys!" I had asked her several times prior to this about going on a team, but at that time she was working full-time as a teacher and was unable to arrange it. Now, however, she had just retired from teaching and, at the last minute (in team-building terms), decided to go with me. It was a rush for her to get all the immunization and planning done, but she made it, and the two of us took off for Ghana on Friday, November thirteenth. We had decided to go in advance of the men so that we could visit the *Project Reach Out Ghana* projects and provide information for *World Hope Canada* on the progress of all the work that we have done as *PROC* and *PROG* over the years. I had been the chairperson of the *PRO Canada* board for twenty-two years, and Kathy had been the secretary for twenty years. We had joined *World Hope Canada* in 2014, and this would be the first time I had gone representing this organization. The work in Ghana is still called *Project Reach Out Ghana,* but *Project Reach Out Canada* is now a part of *World Hope Canada.*

A few weeks before we were to leave, I dropped a large piece of wood on my foot and caused a serious injury to my toe, making it difficult for me to walk. It was uncertain if I'd be able to do the walking necessary in Ghana, but with soaking my foot every day, and wearing protective padding—and really old shoes—I was able to make do.

The team was led by Dan Margeson and Larry Mack; with Jeff McKenna, Chris Hearne, and Keith Krieger as team members. I did make it known that I was used to being the leader, and might get a little bit bossy—so for them to be aware. Because I had been to Ghana so many times, I had specific cultural information that others might not have, and I might offer my opinion without thinking once in a while. (Those who know me know I can do this often under normal circumstances!)

Getting pushed out of the ditch

Kathy and Bensah, her sponsored child

Kathy and I stayed in the guest room at Joe and Jemima Ocran's. We shopped for things for the Ghana Market to sell in Canada, bought the medicines for the clinics that we planned to do in the north, visited Wesleyan Academy (Anum School), went to the Klefe Vocational School, and also made a visit to Kathy's *Compassion Canada* sponsored children. One, a boy named "Bensah" lived in Vome, a place that was very difficult to find. The road was absolutely terrible. Trying to avoid the potholes, we slid into a ditch and had to be pushed out.

The story of the second time we went into the ditch is much too long to go into. Suffice it to say there was no one—no houses, and nothing to help us—until a man with a cell phone came along on a bicycle. He was able to get us help. After a long time, we were out of that mess.

Kathy and Angelina, her sponsored child.

On Thursday, November nineteenth we drove to visit Angelina, Kathy's second *Compassion Canada* sponsored child. Joe was not feeling well, so he didn't go with us. Samuel, the *PROG* projects officer, went with us. We went to Angelina's school where five hundred sixty students attend. While Kathy was visiting with Angelina, and I was taking pictures, I took a drink from a can of pop; when I put my head back, the vertigo, with which I had been having a problem, caused terrible dizziness, and I fell to the ground—cutting my arm, legs, and head, and breaking my glasses. That was the only time I ever had a serious fall in Ghana to date. I did some first-aid on myself, and we went on with the visit.

Friday we caught up on all the things that needed to be done: laundry, unpacking all the medications, checking items against the invoice, and tearing up cotton sheets to be used as bandages for injured feet and legs. Saturday we visited Ashiyie Clinic, and showed the staff how to do the Epley procedure for vertigo. We then went on to the Ayikume farm. It had rained and we got stuck in the lane to the farm. That made three times we had been stuck in the mud that week.

The men arrived on Saturday night from Canada, and we all went off to church at Ashalley-Botwe on Sunday. Because we couldn't take the large suitcases and the boxes of medications on the plane to the north, everything was packed into the van so that the driver, Bernard, and Pastor Kwame Frempong would be able to start the long drive to the north early Monday morning.

Monday morning, November twenty-third, we flew Africa World Airlines from Accra to Tamale. The trip that takes between twelve and fourteen hours by car, takes only forty-eight minutes by plane. Our van made it to Tamale, and we rode into the city. Pastor Addison was at the bus station and he took all our luggage on the bus while we drove to Salaga on the 'shake, rattle, and roll' road. Joe had reserved a new hotel for us and had made a down payment, but when we got there, they had rented all our rooms to someone else. So...after we waited—in the dark outside with the mosquitoes—they finally found us a place to sleep in a very dirty house that had no electricity—which meant no fans. I sprayed everything with Raid and Lysol. We opened the windows and didn't unpack except for sheets, towels and night wear. After a very uncomfortable night, we woke up to power on but water off. After breakfast, they made the rooms we had originally rented available to us, and we moved in. The hotel was new, clean, had air-conditioning and was comfortable, but (there is always a "but") our door wouldn't lock. They tried to fix it, but we had to take our valuables with us each day and prayed that everything else would be safe with the man who was supposed to be the guard of the compound.

Kathy and I sorted the medications into five different piles for the five clinics that we were planning. The men went off to the Salaga guest house where they would be working for the next week. Our meals were being catered by Francis, a pastor friend of Joe's, who had cooked for Westerners in the past. All the food was good. Kathy and I made our own lunches as we were going to the villages.

Our first clinic was held on Wednesday at Opando. We had our scholarship nurse, Ibrahim, and Dawuni, a physician's assistant from Yendi, assessing people. Kathy helped by taking temperatures and kept about seventy noisy children amused. We treated one hundred twenty-seven people. On Thursday we travelled to the village of Buobang. Ibrahim, the nurse, was sick

The team with Francis and his wife (the caterers)

but he kept working. With the two nurses, we changed the way we were running the clinic. Kathy and Dawuni saw all the children and Ibrahim and a local translator saw all the adults. It was much more organized. We were able to treat two hundred and nine people. When we had a flat tire on the way home, Pastor Addison came along on his motorcycle, and I convinced him to take me to the hotel on his motorcycle. It was not the most graceful mount, but it was better than the attempted dismount! When we got to the hotel, I couldn't get off. Finally, a couple of the other guests came along and helped me off.

Friday night the power went off, so it was a hot night. We took the men to the guesthouse and we headed for Bukyondu. We set up the clinic in record time and treated two hundred fifty-eight people; however, there were still some we couldn't get to. My vertigo was acting up again, and I had to hold on to people when walking so I wouldn't fall. Pastor Jacob interpreted for me at the medication table, and he wouldn't let me go anywhere without holding on to me.

Saturday was sort of a day off to get caught up on many things that needed to be done. The power was off. Francis took us on a tour of Salaga, where the slaves used to be brought in from other areas, sold on the slave market, and taken from there to

Cape Coast, to be put on the ships for the New World. We went to the slave baths, and the slave market, and drove around the market area. We did a bit of shopping and laundry. Dan came by our room to have three ticks removed. Joe, Larry, Bernard, the driver, and Pastor John all came back from Tamale where there had been a Northern Pastors meeting. Francis was able to buy extra units for his modem so that we could plug in my laptop and send e-mails to our families back in Canada. Up until now, we had been unable to contact them to let them know we were alright.

The 2015 team: Jeff McKenna, Chris Hearn, Keith Krieger, Dan Margeson, Larry Mack, Kathy deSouza, Carole Tanney, and Joe Ocran

Each day, Kathy and I made sandwiches to have for lunch, and Francis provided a wonderful fruit salad for us. Sunday we headed for Kabeso for church. The road was terrible, and it took a long time to get there. We were able to give out the dresses that the Sew and Sews in Brockville had made, as well as give out the kits of reusable sanitary pads. We didn't have enough, but gave out what we had to the young women there and explained how to use them.

After lunch, we drove on to the village of Kekpeni. Dan had been there on a previous mission trip and he wanted to see it again. A bad storm had taken down the corner of the building,

The outside of the Salaga guest House

but they still held church in the building. Between two and three hundred people showed up for an impromptu service. On the way back to Salaga, we came upon a funeral procession. The burial had just taken place and the people were having a huge celebration with lots of dancing—which took up the road—so we sat and watched.

Monday, November thirtieth we dropped off the construction team at the guest house. The hydro poles were in, as were the lines up to the house. We headed out over the same terrible road to the village of Loloto. The clinic started slowly, but people kept coming,—about three hundred of them in all.

We actually treated two hundred and thirty-nine people. We saw the usual things at these clinics: hypertension, malnutrition. malaria, worms, upper respiratory infections with bad coughs, arthritic pain, chest and neck pain, headaches, and open sores We saw many pregnant women and small babies. At this clinic, we saw a child with what appeared to be cerebral palsy.

It was a cool twenty-six degrees Celsius on the Tuesday morning; the coolest yet, but by the afternoon it was back up to over thirty-six. After dropping the men off at the guest house, we headed off to the village of Bakotido, only ten minutes away from Salaga. There is no Wesleyan church there, but it is near Pastor Jacob's village, and he is friends with the pastor of the Evangelical Church here. The clinic ran very smoothly. We treated two hun-

The construction team and their Ghanaian helpers

dred thirty-four people, and Kathy was able to give out clothes made by the Sew and Sews. We also gave out small toy bears, and baby blankets for a thirteen-day-old baby, and four other babies under one month old.

We saw a woman with a large growth on her neck. We paid for her to go to the hospital for medication that we didn't have. We saw a girl with ringworm on her legs and back, and treated several eye and ear infections. A total of one thousand sixty-six people were treated by our medical team at five village clinics.

On our way back to Salaga, we got a tour of the guesthouse on which the men had been working. The electricity was on and working and all the ceilings were done. The back and front door frames were finished and stained with the doors hung. The security bars were being installed on the windows. All the rooms, and two-thirds of the outside walls, were parged. The house has four, twelve-foot by twelve-foot bedrooms with bathrooms, a sixteen-foot by twelve-foot living room, a sixteen-foot by eight-foot dining room, a sixteen-foot by nine-foot kitchen, two long halls, a pantry, and a bathroom. There was still much to be done. The floor would be expensive. They needed a well, a septic system, plus all the furnishings and a wall around the compound.

Wednesday, December second we headed back to Tamale to the airport, only to find out, after a long wait, that the flight was cancelled due to dust and sand in the air from the Harmattan, the wind that brings the sand from the Sahara desert. It was not safe for the plane to fly. After a lot of readjusting of the luggage, it was decided that Kathy and I would take the State bus to Accra, and the men would squeeze into the van and drive home. Others had the same of idea of taking the bus, and we had to wait until the last bus of the day that would travel all night.

Jemima had told me, years before, that the night bus was very dangerous, as men sometimes stopped the bus in the night and robbed the passengers. We had to take the seats at the rear. The engine was right beneath the seats, which made them very hot. Every time we hit a bump in the road, the bus bounced, and we hit our heads on the ceiling. The driver didn't stop at the special bus stops along the way, but had pit stops along the road, during the night.

We arrived in Accra at four a.m., but the bus depot was closed. They let us out at a taxi station. With a lot of emergency prayer, we looked around and saw a clean-cut-looking taxi driver, and asked him if he would drive us to Tema. When we got in the taxi, he was playing Christian music, and was a very nice man. When we got to Joe and Jemima's home, Jemima had been up all night praying that we would be safe. The van with all the men didn't arrive until late in the evening on Thursday. They apparently did some sightseeing in Kumasi on the way home.

Friday, December fourth was our last day in Ghana. We did some last-minute shopping and packing, and left for the airport; only to find that the motorway, the fastest way to the airport, was closed—so we had to take the Spintex Road with very heavy traffic. We were late to check in, but we made it.

This trip we went Air Canada and British Air, so had a long layover at Heathrow Airport where I was able to do all my accounting for the Ghana Market things and write my reports. Uneventful flight from Heathrow to Ottawa. Thanking God for another successful visit to Ghana.

Reflections from Kathy deSouza

"This 2015 missions trip was a life-changing experience for me. It was my first trip to Ghana. Although I was involved as part of the *Project Reach Out Canada* board and had heard all about the projects in Ghana, it was amazing to actually meet the people, and see the impact the churches and projects were having on the lives of the people. There was no way to prepare for the bumpy, dusty, red-clay roads; the extreme heat, and the degree of poverty that we saw in the villages of Northern Ghana; yet we saw joy in the faces of the people as they sang, prayed, danced, and praised God in the church services. It was a brand-new experience for me to help with the medical clinics held under mango trees in each village, and to sing and dance with the children. I enjoyed travelling and sharing meals with the great team of men who were working on the guesthouse in Salaga (Chris, Jeff, Dan, Keith, and Larry). It was an incredible trip, and I am thankful that God called me to go and to have a part in his work in Ghana."

Reflections from Jeff McKenna

"In 2015, as a new Christian, I was baptized. Only a few months later, when the first notice for a missions trip to Ghana was given during a Sunday morning service at a Wesleyan Church in Ottawa, the pastor who led the project, Rev. Larry Mack, mentioned he was looking for masons and people skilled in carpentry. I immediately looked at my then-to-be wife and told her I had to go. At this point in my life, I had been through three different careers: Journalism, Masonry, and Carpentry. And up until my trip to Ghana, I had believed that every one of these careers led to a dead end, a failed path in life, and I was lost.

"My skills as a mason were put to use immediately, and my skills as a carpenter/furniture maker would later be useful during my future trips. Eventually, I learned that these paths were not "failures" at all, but were in fact carefully made plans, and catered exactly to the future God had in store for me.

"God has given us all a plan, and although we may not understand the details, we must trust that it is all being done for a reason.

"During the missions trip (which was my first trip out of North America), I discovered what it feels like to see someone who has so little, but is so happy. Sunday morning church service lasts all day there; it's not the forty-five minutes that we're used to. People are always in conversation and fellowship with one another.

"Going to Ghana also taught me the value of money. It is given to us by God with the intention of spreading it responsibly, giving it to those who truly need it, and not worrying about what we have or need. This trip has given me another career path. I feel God leading me to start studies towards eventually becoming a minister."

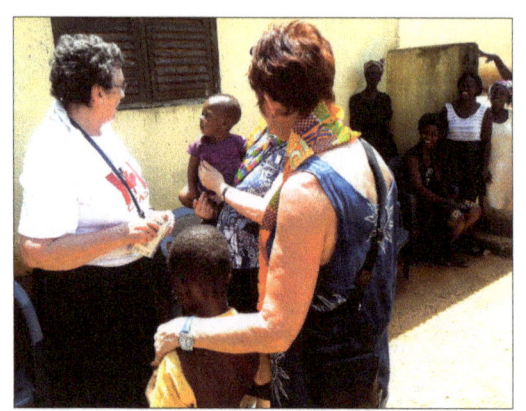

Chapter 27

Two Tiny Problems

A mother stood at the edge of a noisy crowd with a small bundle wrapped in a piece of cloth, her tear-filled eyes begging me to help her. As she unwrapped the cloth, a small, very thin leg protruded—then a very tiny, naked, and emaciated body of a one-month old baby boy, lay exposed.

The baby's skin was so dehydrated that it was wrinkled and peeling. Through the interpreter, the mother said that the baby was feeding poorly; cried all the time, and was "running," interpreted as having diarrhea. What to do? Without intervention, this baby would die within a day or two. In Ghana, fifty-one out of every one thousand live births die before their fifth birthday. If she were in Canada, the mother would take the baby to the hospital, where he would go into a neonatal, intensive-care unit, have an intravenous started, and receive expert pediatric care.

There was no doctor for this clinic, so the nurse prescribed a few drops of an infant antidiarrheal medication to be given with every feeding, to encourage the baby to breast-feed more often. Additionally, the nurse directed the mother to give a few spoonfuls of rehydration salts that had been reconstituted in boiled water, between breast-feedings.

Did this baby survive? We don't know. We were at her village for a four-hour day clinic held under the large mango tree that served as the village meeting place, and there was no way to follow up. He surely would have died, if we had not been there that day. We prayed that the simple treatment prescribed would be the treatment that stayed his deteriorating condition and gave his body the opportunity to heal itself.

There is no access to local medical care without a long trip over horrendous roads to a district hospital or health clinic, assuming that there would be some type of transportation and that the woman had a few extra coins to be able to pay at the hospital. Not all medical care is covered by the new government medical plan, and she probably was not registered anyway.

I put a little skull cap hat on the baby, and wrapped him in a small blanket, both made by a group of women in Brockville, Ontario. I gave the baby a kiss, and the woman thanked me with a kiss on my hand as she walked away clutching the medicine. I thought of my healthy grandsons in Canada receiving unbelievable medical care, and prayed that this tiny baby boy would survive to reach the potential that God had for his life.

Another clinic, another mother, another baby. The mother didn't even present the baby to the doctor. She registered herself, and when she came to the medication table for me to fill her prescription, she opened the cover on the small package she was carrying—and there was an emaciated, dehydrated baby! At first glance, I thought the baby was dead—and then he took a shallow breath. I did a quick examination and realized there was nothing we could do. She said he was two-months-old and wasn't feeding well. I prayed for the baby and then asked the mother to go home and prepare to take the baby to the hospital with us when we left for the day. At the end of the clinic, she was there with the baby. We picked up the father and took them to the hospital.

When we arrived, the physician's assistant who was working the clinics with us, Pastor John, and I went with the parents for the baby to be

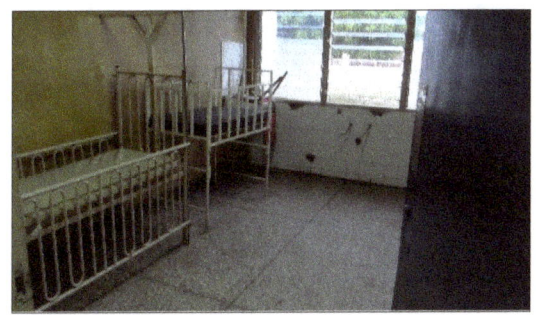

Cribs in the hospital at Yendi

seen. Having a white person accompanying her turned out to be an advantage as we went to the head of the line at every stop. The rest of the team went back to the hotel. The baby was seen, and weighed in at two-point-two kilograms (just over five pounds); was tested for malaria, diabetes, parasites, and had blood work done. All these tests had to be paid for. He was admitted to the hospital and we were given a list of medications and other items that were needed for his care. We went into the city to buy the items and came back to the hospital. The father had a medical care card; this was for the new health care scheme that had recently been instituted in Ghana. It provided for the bed and the care of nurses and doctors, but not for the medicines or the items needed for his care.

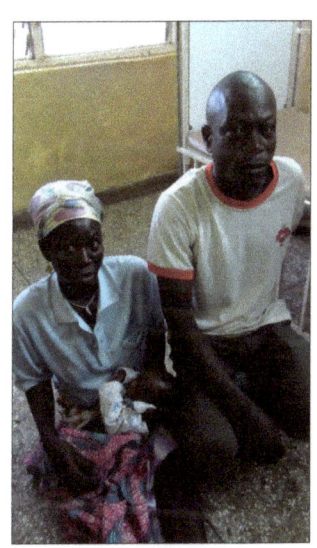

Baby Athassah and his parents

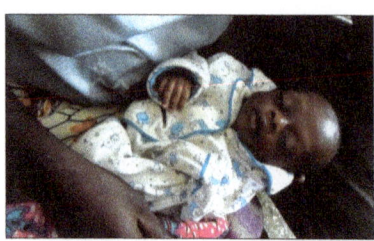

Baby Athassah four days after treatment began.
Mother's name Ngiuyeyo;
Father's name Alasan;
Family name Bidakdin

The baby boy, named Bidakdin (family name) Athassah (given name), was assigned a crib with five other cribs in a small room. There were no chairs for the parents; no bedding, just a crib. The parents of all the children were sitting on the floor with their babies in their arms.

A nurse tried to start an intravenous using the baby's foot. It was unsuccessful twice; but on the third try, after getting a smaller IV set, they were able to get it started. The baby was trying to cry, the mother was crying, and I was crying. When they finally got the IV in, I loudly said, "Thank you, Jesus. I prayed so hard." All the families that were waiting were looking at me, and then I realized that they were all Muslims.

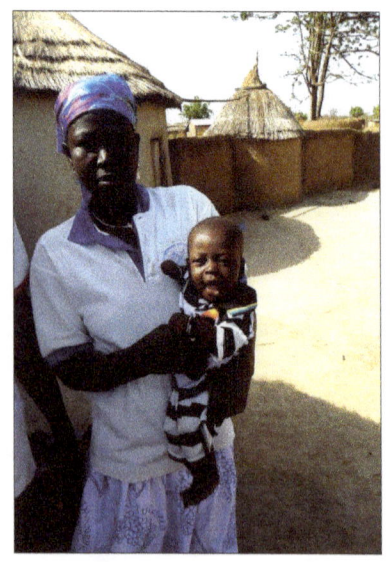

Mother slept on the floor and father slept outside in the walkway. Dad was given money from our team funds for food. The team went to the hospital every evening, after the remaining clinics, to see the baby and pray for him and his parents. The mother and baby were given nutritional counselling, and the baby was given the antibiotics we had purchased. He was started on a formula supplement. After four days hospitalization, the little family was discharged and went back to their village on a trotro, the local bus.

Does a one day clinic do any good? Ask these parents. Another life saved, and even if it was the only one in all the clinics held over the years, it would be worth all the expense and time.

A month after we got home to Canada, I was talking to Joe Ocran and asked about the little boy. He said the report from the pastor was that he was doing well.

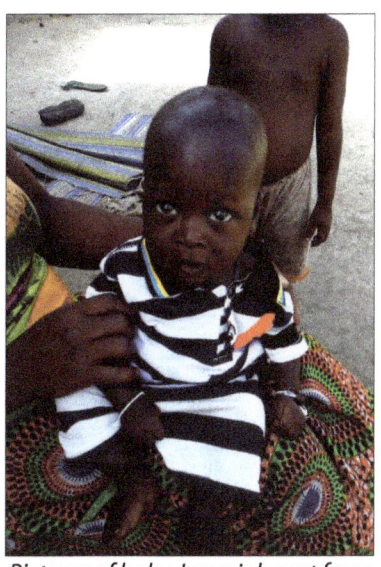

Pictures of baby Jeremiah sent from Ghana in March, 2019

Three months later, we had an e-mail from Pastor John saying that the parents wanted the team to give the baby a Christian name. We chose Jeremiah from *Jeremiah 29:11*: "For I know the plans I have for you, declares the Lord, plans to prosper you and not to harm you, plans to give you hope and a future." Thank you Jesus!

Chapter 28

I Can't Find My....
2017

On Friday, May 2017, Kathy deSouza, Ginny Davis and I headed to Montreal via Ottawa, then on to Amsterdam and Accra. The extra three suitcases each for our team seemed to be a challenge for the KLM agent that checked us in, but we finally got it done. We somehow got separated before boarding, and Ginny and I went to the wrong boarding area. Ginny had hurt her foot a couple of weeks before we were to leave and was having difficulty walking, so we took a ride on a people mover and just made the boarding area before they were to close the door. Having no idea where we were, Kathy was starting to panic. Never again will we separate. We'll wait for each other and go on together.

The flight was uneventful. Kathy wanted to rest at the airport, so Ginny and I went into the city and took a canal tour. There are a lot of regulations involved in leaving the airport and getting back in. You have to go through all the searches et cetera, as if you were just arriving to catch a regular flight. It used to be a lot easier, so I may not take other groups into Amsterdam another time. When we went to board the flight to Accra, we had to surrender our carry-on luggage as there wasn't enough room for everyone's luggage on the plane. When we got to Accra, we got through customs with no problems but had to wait for one hour and fifteen minutes to get all our nine big suitcases and three carry-ons. During all that time Joe, Jemima, and Mikel had to wait. We were to be staying at the Chesterfield Hotel. Very tired.

Sunday, May seventeenth there was a terrible storm with high winds and heavy rain. Frank, our driver, drove the car right up to the doors so we could go to church. Two pastors from Liberia were visiting. Rev. James, the president of the Wesleyan Bible College in Liberia, preached. There was a leadership conference in Winneba. Joe was off for that late Sunday afternoon.

Monday, May eighteenth we headed to Accra to get the medicines for the planned clinics and to get money changed. It took a lot longer than was planned and I spent time visiting with the manager of the bank while Samuel, the *Project Reach Out Ghana* projects manager worried about where I was. Then on to Community One market to get fruits and vegetables and to shop for things that we sell at the Ghana market in Canada. I still hadn't gotten turned around in my time and energy from the trip. Tuesday we headed for Anum to visit the Wesleyan Academy. Only one hundred thirty students were registered. We donated all the school supplies and library books we brought and gave gifts to the students—dolls and matchbox cars to the younger kids, and reusable sanitary products to the older girls and

Filling the medication order at the pharmacy warehouse.

female teachers to help them stay in school. We gave hankies to the boys and pens to the male teachers. On to Klefe Vocational School. We got stopped three times by the police for the license plate not being in the right place and had to pay an "unofficial" tax. When it came time to eat, we couldn't find our lunch; it had been left behind by mistake—but we had bread and peanut butter. A long day, but it was all made better by a lovely dinner at Jemima's.

The women carry the boxes to our car on the heads

One of the jobs—a big job—that had to be done, was to check all the medicines we bought against the invoice that we paid. There is always something, often many somethings, that are missing. This was to be a rest day but we were still working. Off to Community One market again, and on to a grocery store. Our breakfasts are provided at the hotel, but we are trying to do our own lunches and dinners as much as we can.

Thursday we headed off to Ashiyie Community clinic to hold a free clinic there. A pleasant surprise when we got there was seeing Dawuni; we called him by his English name, "Daniel." He had worked with us three times before, and was so talented. He speaks twelve languages and dialects and is a physician's assistant. We know how he does things, so it is a bonus to have him for our medical person at clinics. The first clinic done every year is always a learning process, and we usually see fewer people. Dr. Gabriel, the Ashiyie doctor, and Dawuni were doing assessments and writing prescriptions; Ginny and Kathy organized the patients, took temperatures, gave out gifts to the children, and took pictures; and I, along with Mabel, the clinic pharmacy tech, filled the prescriptions. Jemima was there helping as well. The Ashiyie clinic continued to see regular patients. We treated one hundred eight people, and donated some medical supplies to the clinic that we had brought from Canada.

One thing that was different this year was that I had to reconstitute pediatric medications. When reconstituting the Ampicillin, I inhaled some of the dry medicine and, with my allergy to Penicillin, I developed an itchy, raised rash on my face and neck. In future clinics, I would have to be very careful doing the reconstituting process.

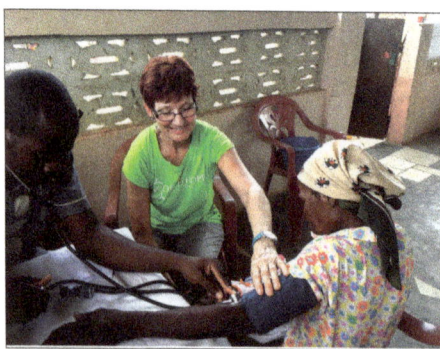

Ginny assisting at the assess-

Friday, May twelfth we headed to Appolonia to do a clinic in this village, where the Wesleyan Church was building a new church funded by the memorial gifts from the funeral of Marilyn

Bertrim. Arrangements were supposed to have been made, but when we got there, no one knew that we were coming.

After talking to the assembly man, he arranged

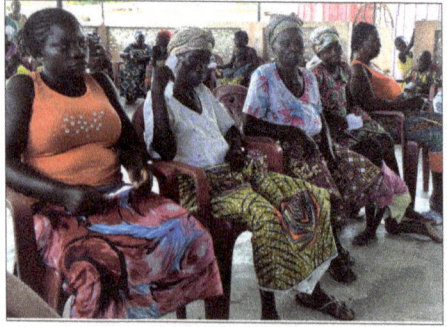

Women waiting to be seen

for us to use a structure in the center of the village. We treated one hundred twenty-three people in thirty-seven Celsius temperatures. We saw many older people with high blood pressure, and many babies as well.

At church Ginny, Kathy and Carole in African dresses

On Mother's Day weekend, before Joe left for the conference, he informed me that I was going to be the speaker for the Sunday morning service. It was a scramble, but with Kathy's help, and the internet helping to find the references I wanted, I was able to put together a "sermon." All women took part in the service and Jemima interpreted for me. After the service, there was a special Mother's day meal at which the men were supposed to serve the women.

Car packed tight

The rest of Sunday was spent packing for our week in the Western Central area of Ghana.

On Monday, May fifteenth we packed up the car and five people and heading for Duakwa. Everyone said we wouldn't fit everything in, but we did. We stopped at Winneba where the conference was being held, and had lunch with Joe, then headed out again.

The temporary Duakwa school. Ages two through six years

I was the only one who had been to Duakwa before, but it was twenty years prior to this visit.

I recognized the area of the church and found it. Joe had made reservations at a resort for us. It was expensive and beautiful on the outside, but lacking on the inside—no light bulbs in the lights, leaking air-conditioners, and no water in the cottage where Kathy and Ginny were to stay. After moving around, we finally got settled in the main building. We ate our breakfasts and suppers there and fixed our own lunches. When we were making the fruit salad, the watermelon exploded. It had been spoiled on the inside!

Waiting for clinic to start

We decided ahead of time that the first day, the clinic would be for the school children, their parents and the people from the church; the second day would be for the people from the village.

The school had sixty-five students with three teachers. The teachers were going to school themselves on the weekends to get their teaching credentials. *PROG* had purchased property on the main road to build a primary school. At the first clinic, we treated one hundred thirteen people, and the second day, one hundred forty five. Our driver, Frank, had family in a nearby village. His mother was very sick, so he took Dawuni to see her. She was diagnosed with cerebral malaria. We purchased special antibiotics for her and they returned to administer them. Two days later, we went to his village and met his mother. She was on her feet and feeling much better.

Duakwa is quite near where my Compassion sponsored child, Ernestina, lived, so on Thursday, May eighteenth we drove there to see her and her family, then drove on to Cape Coast to do a bit of sightseeing. We stayed at the Almond Tree Hotel, which is owned by the niece of a couple who live in Brockville. It had an ocean view, much to Ginny's pleasure. She loves the water and walks on the beach as often as she can. On Friday we went on a tour of the slave castle at Cape Coast. After the tour, Kathy was unable to find her phone.

Ernestina, my sponsored child, with us

We searched everything and everywhere, even going back to the castle. We found a restaurant and gift shop that funds a charity for disabled people with its profits. We had lunch there while Kathy used their Wifi to try and find her phone, even calling her son in Canada to ask for his advice. After much searching, the phone was found in a bag that had already been searched, and we went back to the hotel.

Saturday, May twentieth we left to return to Tema via Accra, stopping to shop for things to bring back for the Ghana market. The trip back had some interesting moments. A caravan of cars led by many police cars with lights flashing, going very fast, flew past us down the center of the highway with traffic coming the other way and everyone trying to get out of their way. It was government dignitaries, maybe even the president, on their way to Cape Coast for a funeral. On the way, Ginny couldn't find her phone (it had fallen out of her bag and was finally discovered under the front seat). It was panic time, as all of her pictures were on it. A big traffic hold up for road pavers at a bridge construction site delayed our trip back to Tema. We needed to make a visit to the dressmakers for some alterations. Heavy rain.

Sheldon Gilmer and Shawn, a man from the University of Ottawa, were in Ghana doing a study on pharmaceuticals. They were staying at the same hotel as us. We had a good visit, and they explained that their study was trying to prove that drug companies were dumping substandard medicines in third world and developing countries. Unbelievable!

Sunday, May twenty-first—my birthday. Exactly twenty-four years ago to the day, I landed for my first trip to Ghana. Jemima had a birthday party for me Saturday night when Joe returned from the conference. He brought Windel Ettienne, from Haiti with him. He was at the conference as well. Sheldon and Shawn from the University of Ottawa were there too. A really different birthday for me!

We attended Ashaley-Botwe Wesleyan Church on Sunday. After church, Kathy gave dresses made by the Sew and Sews in Brockville to girls that Priscilla Frempong had identified as needy. I gave out the packs of reusable sanitary pads to girls who were in school. We then headed back to the hotel. Ginny couldn't find her phone again. After another frantic search, she remembered that she had had it in the car, so we contacted Kwame Frempong and he found it in his car. She had left it there on the way home from church. Another disaster averted!

Monday we went back to Community One market to shop for fabric to make bags and aprons to take back to Canada. Ginny wanted to get her hair done in braids, so she bought extensions and went off to a hairdresser when we got back to the hotel. The results were not good because of her white scalp and too short hair, so they decided not to finish them. We packed suitcases of things to leave in Ghana and suitcases to take home. The power was off for three hours, but we got packed up.

Tuesday, May twenty-third was going home day. We had to check out of the hotel, so we went to Joe and Jemima's. On the way, we were stopped by the police again for the license plates being in the wrong place. The officer was young and trying to make a name for himself. He said the driver disrespected him as a professional and he was going to take him to the police station. I was angry and got out of the car and gave him a tongue lashing, saying he was disrespecting us as professional visitors to his country, helping his people. I even gave him a poke in the chest which everyone in the car thought was hilarious. Guess I could have ended up in jail, but I was angry enough that I think I scared him. Anyway, he let us go on. Sheldon and Shawn left today on British Air. There was a terrorist attack in London so there was concern that they might not be able to go into the city as they had planned.

The first half of our trip home was uneventful, but on the last leg of our flight, a woman got up to the washroom and came back smelling strongly of perfume. Ginny's allergies kicked in, and she had to be moved. She took Benadryl and was fine after an hour or so. We landed safely in Montreal and went on to Ottawa, where and Betty and Don Weatherhead and Gilian Van Dort met us. Safely home!

Ginny loved the ocean

Chapter 29

Twentieth Trip 2018

Thursday, November first, 2018—the first day of my twentieth trip to Ghana.

At lot has happened over the last year: I sold my house where I lived for fifty-three years and moved to Calgary, Alberta (drove by myself almost four thousand kilometres). I now have an apartment just two blocks from my daughter Lana, her husband, Graeme, and my three grandchildren; Lauryn, Oakley, and Harrison.

In August, 2017 while visiting Calgary I met a girl, Catherine Brown, at church. She expressed an interest in going to Ghana, so after a year of talking and planning we headed off on KLM for a direct flight from Calgary to Amsterdam. In Amsterdam, we met up with Kathy deSouza

The 2018 team: Kathy deSouza, Carole Tanney, Catherine Brown and Leree MacPherson

from Brockville, and Leree MacPherson from Oshawa. The four of us traveled on to Ghana. When we arrived at the beautiful new international arrival section of the airport, we had to wait for our luggage. Leree was the only one to have to open her bags and show proof of immunization. (If you can't prove your immunization for yellow fever, you're sent back home on the next flight.) Arrival procedures had been ramped up since my last trip. We had to be fingerprinted and have eye scans and pictures taken—a sign of our times I guess.

This trip, we were staying with Joe and Jemima Ocran in their beautiful new home. It took them twenty years to build it and was worth the wait. In Ghana, it is very unusual to get a mortgage at the bank. The interest rates, sometimes as high as twenty-five percent, are so high that ordinary people can't afford them. You have to build as you can pay, but when you are finished, you own your home outright.

November is the start of the Harmattan season and it is usually very hot, thirty-five to forty degrees Celsius most days. We were very thankful that the Ocrans had a generator so that the fans could run when the power was off. They have a large water tank, which they fill every night, so that if the water goes off while they are asleep, they have water in the morning. Their new home is in Ashalley-Botwe. Since 1990 they have lived in Tema, so it was very different for me, as I was used to getting around Tema and knew where to shop. Jemima cooked for us while we were in Southern Ghana so we had terrific meals. I didn't lose weight as I normally did when I visited Ghana!

The first week in Ghana, we planned to shop for the Ghana Market, visit the *Project Reach Out Ghana* projects that were still running, and get organized to travel to northern Ghana. We unpacked barrels that had been shipped in the summer from Canada, to have things that we needed in the north. The Wesleyan Academy in Anum has one hundred fifty students and fourteen teachers this year. We donated the books and school supplies that we had brought from Canada, and then went on to Klefe Vocational School near the city of Ho, in eastern Ghana. Most of the students were on "Attachment," where they go to businesses in the area and work free to get experience in their programs. We saw the sewing/dressmaking students and gave them all the reusable sanitary pad packages. The trip purchase to Aburi, the carving village, was very interesting. We were able to get some beautiful wood and fabric items for the Ghana Market in Canada.

Leree, Carole, Kathy and, Catherine with the assistant principal at Anum

Thursday, November eighth we flew to northern Ghana. The van, with all of our supplies, left on Wednesday, so that they would be there when arrived. We landed at one-forty-five, and spent the afternoon at pharmaceutical companies, trying to purchase the medications we would need for our clinics. In the past, we have always bought them in Accra and transported them in the van to, the north. Maybe we should have done that again this time, as there were many things we could not get at a good price. Frustrating business! We continued on to Yendi, arriving in the dark—which is not a wise thing to do in northern Ghana. The hotel was nice, but the lights attracted many bugs inside and outside the rooms. One was so large that Catherine swore it was a black crow with a beak! We ended up sealing the windows with tape to help keep the bugs out. Friday it was back to Tamale, about an hour-and-a-half drive, to try to purchase the medications we needed again. In the evening we sorted and checked the medicines, making boxes for each of the five clinics that we planned.

Pastors Solomon and Amos receiving their "pastors' wives blessing bags" from Kathy

Saturday, November tenth we headed off for the village of Oseido, population nine hundred. We had to drive through the river, and then on a motorbike path through the tall grass and crops. We registered one hundred twenty people. This year we had malaria testing kits, as well as a glucometer. Catherine is a microbiology tech in a lab in Calgary, so she was able to do that testing at each clinic which was a big asset. Instead of guessing if people had malaria, we were able to test and give them the appropriate medicines. Sunday we headed for the village of Kutuli for a rousing church service, with fifty to sixty people and lots of singing and dancing. Pastor

Amos is the pastor of this church, and Pastor Solomon from the Saboba church was there also. (Two weeks after we returned home to Canada, Pastor Solomon died of typhoid fever. A great loss!) His sermon was about being a true reflection of God in your community; being a magnet, drawing others to Christ. Kathy gave out clothes made by the Sew and Sews in Brockville to girls who the women leaders of the church identified as being needy. I gave out the sanitary pad packs to girls eleven to eighteen-years-old who were in school.

Monday, Joe headed off to Tamale for a northern pastors' meeting, but Pastors Philip and John stayed with us as interpreters. We went to the village of Katinguli. This is the village where the chief proposed marriage to me in 2014! It was decided to use Leree's work skills from her job in an emergency department of a hospital. She would do triage, so that the clinic time would not be clogged with people who were not really sick, but just wanted to get free medicine. As a result, we treated ninety-seven people who really needed care. Kathy went with a women's leader from the church to give out clothes to needy kids.

A woman presented at the clinic with a tiny baby that I thought was dead when I first saw him. She said he was two months old. He was very dehydrated and barely breathing. For a complete record of this baby's treatment, read the account in Chapter Twenty-Seven, titled "Two Tiny Problems." Tuesday, November thirteenth we were off to Nandundo, Pastor John's village, population over two thousand. (This is the same village that was mentioned in Chapter Twenty-Four about my presence at the first service under a tree.) It was a very noisy, hot, and busy clinic. Kathy was mobbed while trying to give clothing to children. It was decided to give the clothing to a woman who is a leader in the church. She would give the clothing to children later. Joe took the van to travel to Tamale, to meet with the leaders of the Burkina Faso church. He was late coming back for us, and we couldn't see any more people as we had run out of many of the medicines for that clinic. During some of the clinics, Kathy went to visit and interview some of the recipients of micro finance loans for *World Hope International (Canada)* to use in their reporting. On the way back to the hotel, we stopped to see the baby at the hospital. He was still very sick, but some better.

Wednesday, November fourteenth we visited the village of Kambordo. We gave out the dolls and cars to the children that were there at the start of the clinic, and things went much better. Pastor Philip took the clothes to the church, and quietly gathered the Wesleyan children and gave out the clothes. That also went better, with no mobbing. Kathy decided to give the children the balloons that we had brought, and that certainly was an exciting time—a big hit with the children and the adults! Someone in the village gave Joe a chicken, a guinea fowl, and some yams as their tithe. He took the chicken back to the hotel cook to make our supper.

Thursday we visited the village of Kutuli, setting up under a tree beside the road; it was very dusty. We saw the same types of conditions. There were fewer pregnant woman, but one had an open sore on her breast that looked like advanced cancer. She had already been seen at a hospital and had been told that there was nothing that could be done. We referred several people to pharmacies for medicine that we didn't have. Our clinics were finished for this trip. We visited the baby at the hospital again, and gave the father more money for food and travel back to their village. Pastor John had made an appointment for us to meet the chief of that whole area, including Tamale. We visited him in his palace, where he asked a lot of questions about what we had done and thanked us for the work we have been doing for his people.

The Stats for the Clinics

The team with the chief

We treated a total of five hundred thirty people: one hundred nine confirmed cases of malaria; sixty-three people treated for diarrhea; ninety-one for "waist pain;" eleven for chest pain; thirty-nine for abdominal pain, headaches, neck and other undiagnosed pain; and thirty-three pregnant women. We gave out a month's supply of multivitamins, B complex, Folic Acid and Iron pills to each pregnant woman, treated eighty-seven upper respiratory infections, eighteen people with sepsis, fourteen with high blood pressure, many with ear and eye infections, coughs, dizziness and skin rashes. Referrals were made to pharmacies for medicines that we didn't have, and to hospitals for treatment

The head matron of the hospital receiving the medications from Pastor John and myself

of high blood pressure, like the man with a BP of two-twenty/one fifty. We also made a referral to Yendi hospital for a very sick baby. The remainder of the medicines that we didn't use were donated to the Yendi District Hospital. With our hotel bill paid and our good-byes said, we headed back to Tamale and on to Mole National Game Park, near Domango, where we registered for the safari for the next day. Because there were no vacancies at the park hotel, we drove back to Domango to stay the night in the "Home Touch Guest House," a less than prime hotel. We left early in the morning for a two-and-a-half-hour safari. Sad to say, we did not see any elephants, but did see many other wildlife. We made a stop on the way back to Tamale at the world famous Larabanga mosque, supposedly the oldest mosque in Africa. After arriving in Tamale and the Radach Hotel, we waited for our flight back to Accra, and the van left for the twelve-hour drive back to Ashalley-Botwe.

Sunday we attended the Wesleyan Church in Asite. The van had a broken belt to the air-conditioner, so we drove two cars; Jemima's, and her brother Seth's car. While visiting after church, we heard thunder in the distance, so we headed back, but got caught in a heavy rain storm. We made many last minute visits to the dressmaker, to the beach, to the market for last-minute purchases, to Sakumono church, to the headquarters building to show the girls, to Dr. Arthur's clinic, and to the GODIA (God is Alive) Clinic, to donate some medical supplies that Leree had brought from Canada. It was then time to start packing for home.

Wednesday, November twenty-first there were lots of last minute things to do. Kathy interviewed another woman who had received a microfinance loan. We had to transfer pictures from cameras to memory sticks, send e-mails, and of course visit a new ice-cream shop with Joe. On the long wait in Amsterdam, we rested for a few hours and then sat and talked, doing our re-entry evaluations (questions about our visit, the best and worse memories, our thoughts, suggestions for improving). Kathy and Leree took off for Toronto and Catherine and I left for Calgary. It was a long, eight-hour flight to Calgary. The complete flight trip for us from Calgary was twelve thousand eighteen kilometres. We had no problems going through immigration or customs with all our "stuff." It was good to see our families and to be safely home again. Thank you Lord, for your protection once again.

Reflections from Leree MacPherson, 2018 Team:

"I had always wanted to go to Ghana, ever since meeting Joe Ocran when I was a kid in Shawville. When I heard that Carole Tanney was planning another trip to Ghana in 2018, I e-mailed her in December, 2017 asking for more information. My heart for missions and my gift of nursing could be combined. I was thrilled.

"Now, I'll be honest—prepping for this trip, I thought we were heading to pre-established clinics to help the physicians and nurses. I was wrong. In reality, our team all piled into our van, and we drove to remote villages and set up our own

Leree ready for a clinic (with the baby goat behind her chair)

clinics under trees. I was surrounded with doubt that the clinics were actually beneficial. How could our team really be significant to everyone's health? How could one course of antibiotics or malaria pills help them for the future? My answer came the next morning at breakfast. Pastor Joe prayed over the food, and then went on to say that the Lord is the great physician, and that He is the one who heals, not our medication. There it was: my medical heart wrecked by the miraculous abilities of Jesus. It was such an eye-opening, humbling, and joyful experience. I couldn't wait to go back and share my gifts again, and learn more from these people. To God be the Glory!

Ghana Reflections (First trip and Second chances) From Catherine Brown, 2018 Team Member

"My Ghana experience began with a 'God-appointed' meeting at Centre Street Church in Calgary in August, 2017. There I met Carole Tanney and learned that she was a nurse and had been taking people on mission trips to Ghana for twenty-five years! Earlier that summer, I had been offered an opportunity to go on a volunteer awareness trip to Malawi, but had cancelled my seat. After the service, before coffee, I had just prayed that God would lead me to another opportunity to go on a mission trip. So, quick prayer, no waiting, instant answer! Wow!

"Travelling to Ghana in 2018 was, for me, the opening of a door to Africa. I had relatives living in Ghana and Sierra Leone when I was a child, and the places held great fascination. My husband grew up in Rhodesia (now Zimbabwe). Visiting the continent was a long-time dream.

"There were many tasks to be done: unpacking previously shipped barrels, organizing medical supplies brought from

Canada, purchasing and allocating medications for clinics to be held. My job at the clinics was collecting finger-poke blood samples for rapid malaria testing, which kept me quite busy. I enjoyed taking photos of the villages and joining in with the children's dances at the end of the clinic day.

Catherine "working"- malaria testing

"Working in the village medical clinics was sometimes eye-opening and challenging. Our team had daily prayers and devotions, and Rev Joe Ocran led us in a very meaningful communion service at our Yendi hotel. Trusting in God was a big part of this trip and His presence was with us, as evidenced with the tiny baby from Katinguli village who was close to death and is now a thriving, happy baby.

"There seems to be great human potential in Ghana. I saw energy, great emphasis on education, entrepreneurship, and spirituality in the people. Church services and village groups of children were full of energy and devotion in their songs and dances. There are many signs for schools and educational institutions, and rigorous curricula in the junior schools seemed to be the norm. Entrepreneurship was evident with the market vendors and street basket vendors, while big industry is booming in the coastal city of Tema. Spirituality was demonstrated in the marketplace, for example, in the playing of traditional Christian hymns and in signs declaring, "Givers Never Lack." That last sentiment is possibly better trusted in a country that may be improving its prosperity while relying on God a lot more than our affluent North American society does. I may not be able to 'convert' people here to that way of thinking, but I hope to carry it into my own life."

Chapter 30

Where to go From Here?

As I sit here thinking about how to finish this book, it is a new year, and my thoughts are going back over the last years and ahead to what the future might hold. It never occurred to me that I would live this long, but then I should have had a clue, as my parents and grandfather all lived long lives.

What does God have in store for me in the future? Today I was reading in the last chapter of John's gospel where Jesus was reaffirming Peter, following his denial of Christ before the crucifixion. Peter had reverted to his original occupation—fishing—and hadn't even been successful at that! He had fished all night and caught nothing. He probably was ashamed, depressed, and feeling useless in the commission that Jesus had originally given him. Often, when we have a time of regret and looking back, we revert to a time and an activity that gives us comfort and peace—some old activity that we once did with competence and pride.

Jesus asked Peter, "Simon, son of John, do you truly love me more that these?" More than fish, more than your past life? The past was familiar, and had been satisfying before Jesus had come and called him to follow Him. What about my past? Do I want to revert to what I accomplished in the past? The same old same old? Granted I have had a terrific ministry in music, in helping others through nursing, and in mission ministry. Am I content to rest on what has already been accomplished—or do I love Jesus more than the accomplishments of the past?

Peter answered Jesus, "Yes, Lord. You know that I love you," and Jesus told Peter to feed His lambs, not his "fish." To me, this means start out small again. Lambs are not full-grown sheep—they are babies; and they need nourishing, guiding, and mentoring. Is this my job for the future? To start anew, mentoring and nourishing?

I have made a new start in my old age. I have left my home of fifty-three years, moved halfway across the country to a new city, a new apartment, a new church, a new and different life. Is God asking me, "Do you still love Me and do you still want to do My work"?

Jesus asks a second time, "Simon, son of John, do you love Me?"

Carole, daughter of Ross and Phyllis, do you love Me and want to follow Me? Then take care of My "sheep," These sheep—who are they in my life? My daughter and her family who live close to me and who I can help when needed; my new neighbours, my new church family, my new community? Yes, Lord, I love you and want to serve You.

A third time, Jesus says, "Simon, son of John do you love Me?" Peter was hurt by the continued question. "Lord, You know all things; You know that I love You."

Carole, daughter of Ross and Phyllis, do you really love Me? I, too, love the Lord and want to continue serving Him.

Whoa! What is this next? Jesus is talking about getting old, and having to have people look after me, instead of me doing things for myself, in verse eighteen. Does this mean that I won't be able to have a ministry anymore? No! Jesus says again, "Follow Me." Jesus doesn't want me to look at others and what they are doing, like Peter looks at John. He wants me to look at Him, and follow Him wherever He leads me. Is this a new ministry or a different way of doing the ministry that I have been doing all my life?

Is it the same or different? In old age we can't always do things as we did when we were young. In music, I was the director, the accompanist, the one making many of the decisions. Now what? I've joined a choir. Now I'm a participant!

In missions ministry, I was a leader, the chair of *Project Reach Out Canada*, serving on boards and committees, leading teams to the mission field. Now, what does the future hold? Here, I am no longer serving as a leader, but encouraging and educating others about the needs, raising money, recruiting volunteers, and giving advice from my expertise and experience. Is this God's plan for my future? Does He want me to be involved in a passive, supportive leadership way?

Psalm 92:12-15 NIV says, "The righteous will flourish like a palm tree." A palm tree is sturdy in a storm, and every part of the tree is used; nothing is wasted or thrown away when the tree is harvested. "They grow like a cedar of Lebanon; planted in the house of the Lord, they will flourish in the courts of our God. They will still bear fruit in old age, they will stay fresh and green, proclaiming, 'The Lord is upright, he is my Rock and there is no wickedness in Him.'"

There it is! God still has a use for me in my 'old age.' It may not be the same and as active as it once was, but He will keep me "fresh and green" and able to serve Him!

Do I still love Him? Yes! Can I still be used? Yes! Maybe not in exactly the same ways but there is still work for me to do!

"Do you love me, Carole?"

"You know that I love you, Lord. You know all things." Help me, Lord to still be able to feed Your sheep, even when I feel inadequate and tired. *Words Fail Me,* Lord, but I know You love me. Help me to learn from Your Word.

Project Reach Out

ORGANIZATION OF *Project Reach Out Canada*
Rev Joe and Jemima Ocran—International Directors
Organized as a charity in Canada in 1990.
Registered as a NGO in Ghana in 1991
Boards organized in both countries.

PROJECT REACH OUT CANADA BOARD MEMBERS

Charter Members:

Bob Castle, Chairperson 1990-1993

Carol Running, Vice-Chairperson 1990-1993

Margaret LaNier, Secretary- Treasurer 1990-1992

David LaNier 1990-1992

Lynn Castle 1990-1993

Rev. Laurence Croswell 1990- 2011

Faye Croswell 1990- ?

Rev. Tim Rounding 1990- ?

Sherrie Rounding-Davis 1990-2010

Carol Freeman 1990- ?

Rod Freeman 1990- ?

Maureen Seabrook 1990- 2009

Ron Seabrook 1990- March 5, 2007

Al and Dawna Scobie 1990- ?

217

Timeline

1993-1997
- First *Project Reach Out* sponsored trip taken by Carole Tanney
- First medical clinic held in 1993—needs prioritized. Started fund-raising for a mobile medical clinic. (It took four years to raise $40,000 Canadian to buy a Mitsubishi van.)
- Vision team in 1994- Rev. Earl Conley and Carole Tanney
- Started taking Ministry teams in 1995
- Anum School started in bamboo and thatch building
  A three-room building was constructed for kindergarten to grade two, with a room being added each year to accommodate the classes needed by students attending the school.
- Pastoral teaching team in February 1996 - Rev. Laurence Croswell and Carole Tanney doing clinics
- Farming project at Otropke with Pastor Joseph Narh started. Adult literacy classes, mostly for women, started in Otropke with Pastor Joseph Narh teaching.
- Scholarship programs established for primary and secondary school
- Shipment of Bibles and books sent from Canada
- Ashalley-Botwe Kindercare School started in the church building—then separate school building built
- A ten-acre plot of land was leased to start the Ayikuma farm
- Mobile Clinic Van commissioned in January 1997 to help with the government sponsored polio vaccination program,

then licensed to visit approximately thirty villages every month, with a target population of 10,000 people. In three years put 150,000 kilometres on vehicle
- 1997 ministry team in July/August
- *CIDA* application for matching funds funding
- 1999 an information gathering team Sheldon Gilmer, Paul Noren and Carole Tanney to Ghana to assess needs for using the *CIDA* funding

2000—2006

- During these years the partnership with *Help the Aged Canada* and *CIDA* provided matching funds for infrastructure development to accommodate programs for the elderly, age fifty and over
- A three room *PRO* headquarters building built on the property of the Sakumono church
- 2000 - First *CIDA* youth intern, Roxanne Struk, agroforestry intern.
- Ashiyie Community Clinic built and open in 2002
- A well was drilled at Ashiyie
- Four satellite clinics built, three in the north and one in the south (two taken over by the government)
- A forty-foot container sent from Canada each year with medical, agricultural, educational and ministry supplies
- Fifteen *CIDA* youth interns worked with PRO in Ghana in gerontology and agroforestry providing education, in advocacy for the elderly programs and expertise in farming.

- A demonstration farm was established with farm buildings and agroforestry
- Cooperative programs were established in twenty-one villages with minimum of ten people in each cooperative
- A Toyota pick-up truck was purchased for the agroforestry program
- Radio broadcast on issues of the elderly done for two years with potential audience of three million people in three languages
- One new classroom added each year to Anum School for total of ten rooms
- Ministry teams were taken in 2000, 2002, 2003, 2004, 2005, 2006, 2007, 2009, 2011, 2014, 2015, 2017, 2018. Besides these team led by Carole Tanney there were teams led by Joan Thomas, John Markus, Janet Roth, Sheldon Gilmer and Sylvia Summers. Several Church Pastoral training teams were also taken as well.
- 2005 - Started over 80,000 tree seedlings—Acacia, Neem, Mango, Teak, Cashew, Mahogany, etc., at the Ayikumi demonstration farm—sold to the government riverbanks reforestation project as well as tree seedlings for sale to the public and for village cooperatives.

2007- 2013

- Dental/Medical Teams treated 1000 people in one week 1997 dental and medical team in Tamale district of Northern Ghana.
- Klefe Vocational School teaching Sewing, Tie-Dye and

Batik, Carpentry, Masonry and Electrical.

- Second building built
- Well-baby clinics and education for the elderly classes continue
- New Edubaise Vocational School started building for computer-training and a library
- Pineapple and mango fruit for sale from the Ayikume demonstration farm.
- Microfinance/ income generation program started
- Wesleyan Academy (Anum School) added a Junior Secondary School (grades seven to nine were added)
- *Project Reach Out Canada* joined *World Hope Canada* in 2017 to be amalgamated with *World Hope International* to partner with *Project Reach Out Ghana* which will stay as its own NGO recognized by the Ghanaian Government.

www.ingramcontent.com/pod-product-compliance
Lightning Source LLC
Chambersburg PA
CBHW042124100526
44587CB00026B/4173